D1058791

INFECTIOUS
DISEASES
OF THE MOUTH

DEADLY DISEASES AND EPIDEMICS

INFECTIOUS
DISEASES
OF THE MOUTH

Scott C. Kachlany, Ph.D.

CONSULTING EDITOR
Hilary Babcock, M.D., M.P.H.
Infectious Diseases Division
Washington University Schoool of Medicine
Medical Director of Occupational Health (Infectious Diseases)
Barnes-Jewish Hospital and St. Louis Children's Hospital

FOREWORD BY
David Heymann
World Health Organization

CHELSEA HOUSE
PUBLISHERS
An imprint of Infobase Publishing

Deadly Diseases and Epidemics: Infectious Diseases of the Mouth

Copyright © 2007 by Infobase Publishing

Chelsea House
An imprint of Infobase Publishing
132 West 31st Street
New York, NY 10001

ISBN-10: 0-7910-9242-9
ISBN-13: 978-0-7910-9242-2

$ 28.75

Library of Congress Cataloging-in-Publication Data
Kachlany, Scott C.
  Infectious diseases of the mouth / Scott C. Kachlany ; foreword by David Heyman.
      p. cm. — (Deadly diseases and epidemics)
  Includes bibliographical references and index.
  ISBN 0-7910-9242-9 (hc : alk. paper)
  1. Gums—Diseases—Juvenile literature. 2. Teeth—Diseases—Juvenile literature.
I. Title. II. Series.

  RK401.K33 2006
  617.6'3—dc22   2006010421

Series design by Terry Mallon
Cover design by Keith Trego

Printed in the United States of America
Bang EJB 10 9 8 7 6 5 4 3 2 1
This book is printed on acid-free paper.

Table of Contents

Foreword

In the 1960s, many of the infectious diseases that had terrorized generations were tamed. After a century of advances, the leading killers of Americans both young and old were being prevented with new vaccines or cured with new medicines. The risk of death from pneumonia, tuberculosis (TB), meningitis, influenza, whooping cough, and diphtheria declined dramatically. New vaccines lifted the fear that summer would bring polio, and a global campaign was on the verge of eradicating smallpox worldwide. New pesticides like DDT cleared mosquitoes from homes and fields, thus reducing the incidence of malaria, which was present in the southern United States and which remains a leading killer of children worldwide. New technologies produced safe drinking water and removed the risk of cholera and other water-borne diseases. Science seemed unstoppable. Disease seemed destined to all but disappear.

But the euphoria of the 1960s has evaporated.

The microbes fought back. Those causing diseases like TB and malaria evolved resistance to cheap and effective drugs. The mosquito developed the ability to defuse pesticides. New diseases emerged, including AIDS, Legionnaires', and Lyme disease. And diseases which had not been seen in decades reemerged, as the hantavirus did in the Navajo Nation in 1993. Technology itself actually created new health risks. The global transportation network, for example, meant that diseases like West Nile virus could spread beyond isolated regions and quickly become global threats. Even modern public health protections sometimes failed, as they did in 1993 in Milwaukee, Wisconsin, resulting in 400,000 cases of the digestive system illness cryptosporidiosis. And, more recently, the threat from smallpox, a disease believed to be completely eradicated, has returned along with other potential bioterrorism weapons such as anthrax.

The lesson is that the fight against infectious diseases will never end.

In our constant struggle against disease, we as individuals have a weapon that does not require vaccines or drugs, and that is the warehouse of knowledge. We learn from the history of science that "modern" beliefs can be wrong. In this series of books, for example, you will learn that diseases like syphilis were once thought to be caused by eating potatoes. The invention of the microscope set science on the right path. There are more positive lessons from history. For example, smallpox was eliminated by vaccinating everyone who had come in contact with an infected person. This "ring" approach to smallpox control is still the preferred method for confronting an outbreak, should the disease be intentionally reintroduced.

At the same time, we are constantly adding new drugs, new vaccines, and new information to the warehouse. Recently, the entire human genome was decoded. So too was the genome of the parasite that causes malaria. Perhaps by looking at the microbe and the victim through the lens of genetics we will be able to discover new ways to fight malaria, which remains the leading killer of children in many countries.

Because of advances in our understanding of such diseases as AIDS, entire new classes of antiretroviral drugs have been developed. But resistance to all these drugs has already been detected, so we know that AIDS drug development must continue.

Education, experimentation, and the discoveries that grow out of them are the best tools to protect health. Opening this book may put you on the path of discovery. I hope so, because new vaccines, new antibiotics, new technologies, and, most importantly, new scientists are needed now more than ever if we are to remain on the winning side of this struggle against microbes.

David Heymann
Executive Director
Communicable Diseases Section
World Health Organization
Geneva, Switzerland

1

An Introduction to Oral Health in America

When do you think the first-ever surgeon general's report on oral health was released? Surprisingly, the first official report on the state of oral health in America was not released until May of 2000 by the 16th surgeon general, Dr. David Satcher.

In his report, Dr. Satcher revealed some surprising facts about oral health in America. Dr. Satcher termed the U.S. oral health problem the "silent epidemic." A major issue that many Americans face is the lack of appropriate dental care and dental insurance. In many places in America, people have to drive for hundreds of miles just to see a dentist. Many states lack even a single dental school to train future dentists. The key points in his 332-page report were:

- Oral health means much more than healthy teeth.

- Oral health is integral to general health.

- Although safe and effective disease prevention measures exist that everyone can adopt to improve oral health and prevent disease, there are still profound disparities in the oral health of Americans.

- General health risk behaviors, such as tobacco use and poor dietary practices, also affect oral and craniofacial health.

Even though most people throughout the world experience some type of dental problem at some time in their life, oral diseases are not often discussed in the press. Many people have heard of asthma, and some of you reading this may even have it. Tooth decay is five times more common in children than asthma. Scientists and doctors are now finding that infections in the mouth often do not just remain in the mouth. Oral bacteria may actually play an important role in causing heart disease. Paying close attention to oral hygiene and taking good care of your teeth are more important than ever, and not doing so can severely impact your overall health.

Education and research are the keys to keeping this epidemic from spreading. Educating children at a young age about potential diseases of the mouth will increase the chance that they practice good oral hygiene habits throughout their lives. Further research and developments in the field of oral health will be just as important as educating the public. During his presentation, Dr. Satcher emphasized the importance of research, stating, "it is important that we continue further research and build the science based on oral health concerns. Such research has been at the heart of scientific advances in oral health over the past several decades. Our continued investment in research is critical to obtain new knowledge about oral health needs if improvements are to be made."

2

An Introduction to Microbiology

Bacteria are everywhere: on skin, in food, and in mouths. They are often thought of as simple, single-celled, disease-causing organisms. Although they are indeed microscopic, bacteria are highly complex organisms that rarely exist as single cells in nature. Of all the bacteria that are known, only a small fraction of them cause disease in humans and other animals. In fact, most bacteria are beneficial and essential for life on this planet. For example, the recycling of organic matter is carried out largely by bacteria, and, very long ago, photosynthetic bacteria called cyanobacteria were responsible for the creation of today's oxygen-containing atmosphere.

Bacteria that cause disease are of the most interest to society because of the negative impact they can have on our lives. Research on pathogenic bacteria includes studying how these microorganisms cause disease and how to prevent or treat the disease. In order to understand how bacteria pose such a threat to humans, it is important to learn about the bacteria themselves.

BACTERIA AS COMPLEX ORGANISMS

Bacteria, or prokaryotes, are single-celled microorganisms that lack a nucleus. This is in contrast to eukaryotic cells, such as our own, which contain a true nucleus. Bacteria inhabit nearly all environments on the planet and are able to grow in conditions in which humans and other animals could never survive. Although bacteria are often thought of as simple organisms that lack cellular **organelles** (the specialized organs of a cell), they are able to carry out nearly all the biochemical processes that humans can, and they possess a wide range of appendages.

Bacterial cells are approximately one micrometer in length (Figure 2.1), which is 1,000 times smaller than the tip of a pencil. Bacteria are typically either rod-shaped (called a bacillus), spherical (called a coccus), or spiral (called a spirillum) (Figure 2.2). To examine what a bacterial cell looks like and is composed of, let's journey into a bacterium starting from the outside.

Bacterial components on the outside of the cell are known as **extracellular**. One extracellular component many micrometers away from the cell wall is known as a **capsule** (Figure 2.3). As the name suggests, a capsule encases a bacterial cell. Bacterial capsules are usually made up of polysaccharides, or sugars arranged in long chains. Bacteria produce capsules for various reasons. For some bacteria, a capsule helps protect it from harsh conditions, such as extreme environments and the human immune system. For example, some capsules are **hydrated** structures (containing water) that help protect bacteria from dry conditions. A capsule can also help bacteria stick to surfaces. Bacteria have evolved and developed many ways of sticking to surfaces; this is an extremely important ability for bacteria to have. Attaching to a surface helps the bacteria invade tissues and cause disease.

Another extracellular component we might run into are tube-shaped appendages called **pili** (pilus, singular) or fimbriae (fimbria, singular) (Figure 2.3). Pili are composed of protein and can be short or very long (many micrometers in length). Pili have two possible functions: helping bacteria attach to surfaces and exchanging DNA. For attachment, the pili act as cables that anchor cells to a surface. Pili often work in sequence with capsules to promote attachment. The second role of pili is in the exchange of DNA during **conjugation**. Conjugation is the process by which one bacterium (a donor) can pass part of its genetic material (DNA) to another bacterium (the recipient). Pili are responsible for connecting and bringing together the donor and recipient cells during conjugation. Conjugation is an important process because

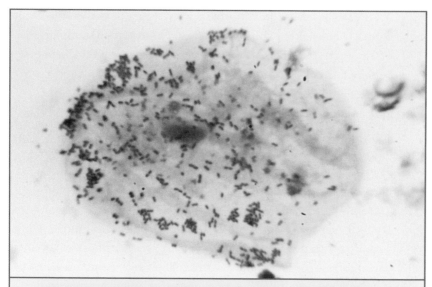

Figure 2.1 This image shows a human cheek cell with many tiny bacteria attached to it. The picture was taken through a light microscope. The bacteria are the small, dark shapes that appear sprinkled over the cell. (Jack Bostrack/Visuals Unlimited)

it allows otherwise **asexual organisms**, such as amoeba or bacteria, to exchange DNA and create genetic variation. Genetic variation allows bacteria to evolve and remain the most successful organisms on Earth. Bacteria can be found in nearly every environment on Earth.

Also on the outside of the cell, **flagella** (flagellum, singular) are flexible, long (several micrometers) **proteinaceous** structures that allow a bacterium to move or swim through different environments (Figure 2.3). Flagella create their force by rotating like a propeller on a boat. Bacteria can even swim in different directions by altering the rotation pattern of their flagella. Bacteria use this motility to go toward food and to steer clear of unappetizing chemicals and compounds.

At the surface of bacteria, we have to distinguish between the two types of cells we are going to examine. The separation of bacteria into two different groups is based on the Gram stain.

The Gram stain technique uses different dyes to "color" bacterial cells either purple or pink when viewed under a microscope. The purple-staining bacteria are called Gram positive and the pink-staining bacteria are Gram negative. The

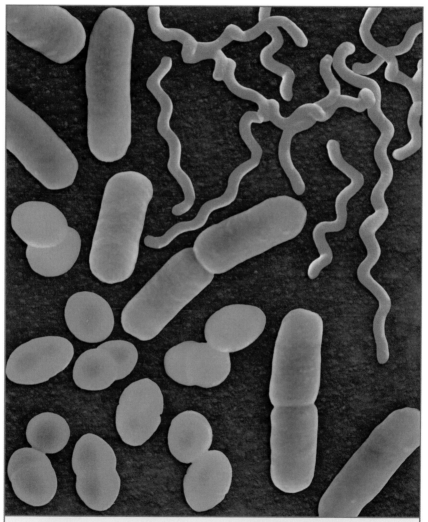

Figure 2.2 This picture was taken through a scanning electron microscope and shows the three different bacterial shapes. From the upper right corner down, they are spirillum, bacillus, and coccus. (Dr. Dennis Kunkel/Visuals Unlimited)

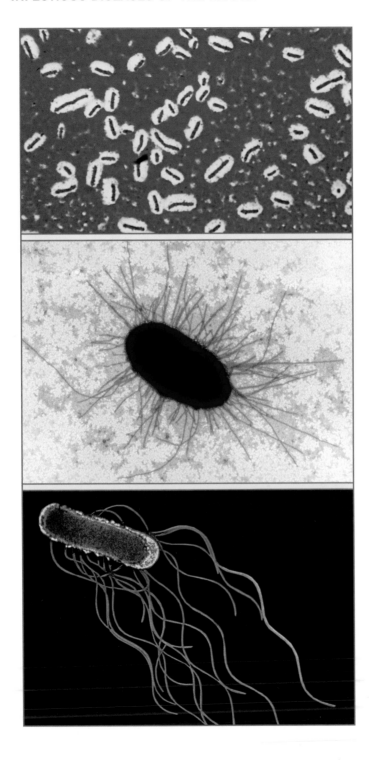

difference in Gram-staining properties between bacteria is due to differences in the composition of their cell surfaces.

The surface of Gram-positive bacteria can be divided into two layers (Figure 2.4). To visualize the outermost layer of the cell, think about a camping tent. Even though the fabric that a tent is made of lacks rigidity, tents come in all different shapes. The way a tent forms its shape is by its strong, rigid rods. In the same way, the shape of a bacterial cell is dictated by a rigid layer called a cell wall (which is actually outside of the rods, unlike some tents). Without a cell wall, a rod-shaped bacterium would be spherical. The cell wall not only gives a bacterial cell its shape and strength, but also it acts as a barrier, protecting cells from toxic chemicals and compounds such as antibiotics.

The cell wall is made up of peptidoglycan. As the name suggests, peptidoglycan is part **peptide** (several amino acids attached to each other) and part **glucan** (sugar). The sugars of peptidoglycan, called N-acetylglucosamine (NAG) and N-acetylmuramic acid (NAM), are attached to each other in a long chain. Many chains are then linked together by peptides that act as bridges, in a process called **transpeptidation** (Figure 2.4). The antibiotic penicillin kills bacteria by preventing the step that links the sugar chains with peptides.

Inside the cell wall matrix resides the cell membrane, which is made up of a **phospholipid bilayer** (containing phosphates and lipids), similar to that of eukaryotic cells. The cell membrane has several important biological properties. First, like the cell wall, it forms a barrier between the inside and outside of the cell.

Figure 2.3 *(opposite page)* This figure shows different bacterial structures. On the top is a light micrograph that shows bacteria that are stained with a special dye to reveal their thick capsules, visible as light areas around the rods. The image in the center was taken with a transmission electron microscope and shows thin pili emanating from a bacterial cell. The figure on the bottom is a transmission electron micrograph that reveals string-like bacterial flagella. (Dr. George J. Wilder/Dr. Dennis Kunkel/Scientifica/Visuals Unlimited)

Hence, the cell membrane lends protection against compounds such as antibiotics. The second essential function the membrane serves is as a site where proteins can function. Important enzymatic reactions, such as respiration, take place at the surface of the membrane. Some proteins are actually inserted within the membrane. These include proteins that are involved in secreting molecules out from inside the bacterial cell. In fact, protein secretion is so important for bacteria to survive and cause disease that many bacteria have multiple **secretion systems**. Each secretion system is composed of many proteins. The proteins of a secretion system assemble together to form, essentially, a channel through which molecules are secreted. Some important secreted molecules that we have already discussed include pili, flagella, and polysaccharide capsules.

The Gram-positive bacterial cell is surrounded by a cell wall layer and a phospholipid cell membrane. Gram-negative cells differ in two important ways: The cell wall of Gram-negative bacteria is much thinner than Gram-positive cell walls, and Gram-negative cells are surrounded by an extra membrane layer on their outside (Figure 2.4). Thus, a Gram-negative cell

GRAM STAINING

In 1884, Danish physician Christian Gram developed a technique to separate bacteria into two groups: Gram positive and Gram negative. In the technique, a purple stain, called crystal violet, and iodine are added to bacteria on a slide. The slide is then washed with alcohol. The cells with a thick layer of peptidoglycan, a polymer consisting of sugars and amino acids, retain the deep purple stain (Gram-positive cells) while the cells with only a thin layer of peptidoglycan lose the stain (Gram-negative cells) and become clear. To make clear cells visible, a red dye, safranin, is added and the result is purple bacteria (Gram positive) or pink bacteria (Gram negative).

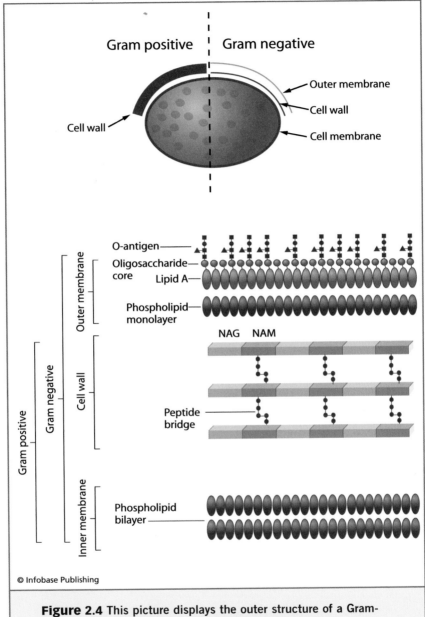

Figure 2.4 This picture displays the outer structure of a Gram-positive and Gram-negative cell. An enlarged view of the membranes and cell wall are diagrammed in the lower image.

has two membranes: the **inner membrane** and the **outer membrane**; the peptidoglycan cell wall can be found between the two membranes.

Unlike the cell membrane of the Gram-positive cell, the outer membrane of the Gram-negative cell is not composed simply of a phospholipid bilayer. Instead, the outermost half of the outer membrane is composed of **lipopolysaccharide**, or LPS (Figure 2.4). LPS itself is composed of three parts, the **O-antigen**, the **oligosaccharide core**, and **lipid A**. The O-antigen consists of several sugar molecules linked together in a chain (the "O" stands for oligosaccharide). This chain of usually four to six sugars constitutes a single unit, and a typical O-antigen is made up of many units (20–50) linked together to form a long chain of repeating units. The word **antigen** is defined simply as a molecule (usually foreign to our bodies) that causes an immune response. Because the O-antigen is the outermost part of the outer membrane and hence exposed on the cell surface, this is what our immune system first "sees" and reacts to when a bacterial pathogen invades our bodies.

Connected to the O-antigen is the oligosaccharide core. The term *oligosaccharide* can be easily defined if we break the word apart. *Oligo-* means "several" and *saccharide* means "sugar." Thus, the oligosacccharide core is a central structure that is made up of several sugar molecules (Figure 2.4). The oligosaccharide core links the O-antigen to lipid A. Lipid A is similar to a phospholipid but lacks the phosphate group. The role of lipid A is to anchor the whole LPS molecule in the outer membrane. LPS constitutes the outer one-half of the outer membrane. The inner half is made up of the standard phospholipid layer.

There are several consequences of having an outer membrane. The outer membrane acts as an extra barrier protecting the cell. The outer membrane also harbors important proteins that help bacteria interact with and sense the external environment and other organisms. This sensing is similar to our own sense of touch. Finally, LPS is an important contributor to the immune response that occurs when bacteria infect our bodies.

Inside the outer membrane is the cell wall. The Gram-negative cell wall is similar to the cell wall of Gram-positive bacteria except that it's much thinner. In fact, in the laboratory, breaking open Gram-positive cells is much more difficult than opening Gram-negative cells.

Inside the cell wall is the inner membrane. Other than relatively minor differences, the Gram-negative inner membrane is similar to the Gram-positive cell membrane.

Finally, beneath the inner membrane is the actual bacterial cell **cytosol**. The cytosol contains the inner components, or guts, of bacteria that are essentially the same for Gram-positive and -negative bacteria. Most people have the misconception that the inside of bacteria is unorganized and sparse. This is not true. Let's examine bacterial guts in more detail.

Although the chromosomes of eukaryotic cells are contained within the nucleus, the single bacterial chromosome is located within the **nucleoid**. The nucleoid is not a true membrane-bound organelle like the nucleus, but rather it is a defined region within the bacterial cell in which the chromosome can be found. A typical bacterial chromosome contains approximately 2 million to 4 million DNA base pairs, depending on the bacterial species.

In eukaryotes, proteins are synthesized on specific organelles called **ribosomes** that reside on the **endoplasmic reticulum**. In bacteria, proteins are also synthesized on ribosomes, except that there is no endoplasmic reticulum. Once proteins are made, they are routed to different places in the cell. Some stay inside the cell and act as structural components or have enzymatic activities that carry out essential biochemical functions for the cell. Other proteins are shuttled to the membrane, where they act as sensors. Still others are proteins that are secreted out of the cell where they act in the external environment. Bacteria have highly coordinated ways of getting proteins and other components of a cell to the right place at the right time. Thus, although eukaryotic cells are larger and appear to have "more" guts, bacteria do the same amount of work that eukaryotic cells do.

It is true that bacteria are only single cells, but human organs such as the heart and lungs are, at their essence, also composed of individual single cells. These cells group together in a highly organized way to form organs that we all can recognize. Bacteria are no different, except that we never think of bacteria as visible to the naked eye or **macroscopic**. But think of what the inside of a toilet bowl looks like if it hasn't been cleaned in a while or how a layer of slime looks floating on the surface of a lake or pond. These formations, called **biofilms**, are composed mostly of bacteria and the products they make. A close look at the scum layer in the toilet or the floating slime on the lake would reveal a network of bacteria organized in pillars and layers, with channels that allow the flow of nutrients and waste. Bacteria can form macroscopic structures that are visible everywhere we turn. The current thinking is that bacteria don't actually live in nature as single cells, but rather in biofilm communities where they interact with other bacteria and microorganisms.

NAMING OF BACTERIA

To continue our discussion of oral bacteria and the diseases some of them cause, it would be helpful to understand how bacteria are named. Bacteria, like all organisms, have two names, just as we have a first and last name. The first name is called the **genus** and the second is called the **species**. A genus is a group of several organisms that are all related to each other, but different. For example, lions, tigers, and leopards are part of the same genus (*Panthera*). The species name refers to organisms that are all of the same type. For example, you and I are both part of the same species (*sapiens*) as well as the same genus, *homo*, which also includes our ancestors, such as *homo neanderthalensis*, or neanderthal man. Two different lions are part of their own species (*leo*), as well as the genus, *panthera*, but tigers, which are also belong to *panthera* are of the species *tigris*. When writing the genus and species name of a bacterium, both names are italicized. The first letter of the genus name is capitalized while the first letter of the species name is lowercase.

The name of a bacterium can sometimes tell you a bit about the organism or the history of the organism. For example, many bacteria are named after the scientist who discovered or studied them. *Escherichia coli* (which can cause food poisoning and urinary tract infections) was discovered by Theodor Escherich in 1888, and *Yersinia pestis* (the bacterium that causes bubonic plague) is named after its discoverer, Alexandre Yersin (1894). Some names reveal the disease they cause, like *Vibrio cholerae* (the cause of cholera) and *Legionella pneumophila* (Legionnaires' disease). Still other names inform us about the shape that bacteria are, as in the genus names *Actinobacillus* (rod-shaped) and *Staphylococcus* (cluster of cocci). Most of the genus and species names of bacteria have a Latin or Greek root, and so deriving a literal meaning can be very revealing.

HOW BACTERIA CAUSE DISEASE

Not all bacteria cause disease in humans. Those that do are called **pathogens**. Each bacterial pathogen has evolved its own way of causing disease in the human **host**. However, most of the disease-causing mechanisms employed by pathogens are similar, and many generalizations can be made. In this section, we will briefly discuss some of the common tools that bacteria use to cause disease. In subsequent chapters, we will discuss how specific bacteria cause specific diseases.

The first step initiating disease is attachment of the bacterium to a surface, called **colonization** (Figure 2.5). For an oral pathogen, the colonization surface might be the tooth or cheek cells. Colonization by bacteria leads to biofilm formation and is an important first step for the bacterium because unattached bacteria are more vulnerable to our body's immune system. Within a biofilm, bacteria can grow and divide in a nutrient-rich environment. The biofilm environment also offers protection

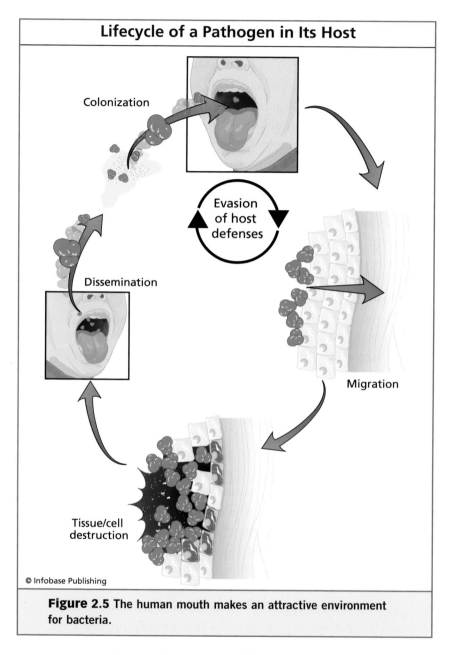

Figure 2.5 The human mouth makes an attractive environment for bacteria.

against the actions of antibiotics and immune cells. Several bacterial products aid in colonization and biofilm formation, including pili, polysaccharide capsules, LPS, and flagella.

After a pathogen colonizes a surface, it often invades deeper into our bodies and spreads to other organs and cell types. The spread of bacteria, or **migration**, can be as simple as moving from one cell to an adjoining cell or as complex as spreading from one cell in the mouth to a completely different cell type in the heart. Migrating to different places in the body gives a pathogen an advantage because it allows the bacterium to "hide" from the immune system and find new sources of food. Bacteria have discovered fascinating ways of hiding, and some become dormant or even invade our own immune cells where they live and grow without being killed. This is similar to a criminal on the loose hiding within a prison.

One way that bacteria hide from the immune system is that the bacteria often become **dormant**. Dormancy is similar to hibernation because it allows the bacterium to remain in the body for long periods of time (sometimes years) without being noticed. During dormancy, the host usually does not experience symptoms of disease. Then, at some later time, the pathogen becomes activated and causes disease. This scenario is true for *Mycobacterium tuberculosis* (the cause of tuberculosis) and many viruses, such as HIV.

Another reason that bacteria spread throughout the body is to acquire nutrients. The mouth, for example, is an extremely competitive environment, with hundreds of different types of microorganisms. With a limited supply of nutrients (especially if you listen to your dentist and don't eat many sweets, which feed bacteria), some bacteria lose out. In an effort to grow and thrive, a pathogen may travel to another part of the body where there is much less competition, such as the heart or lungs.

Next, pathogenic bacteria invade their target cells. Many invasive bacteria produce proteins, called **invasins**, which assist the invasion process. Some invasins help bacteria form holes in the surfaces of host cells while others help turn down the immune response within the cell that is being invaded. Meanwhile, to move from one part of the body to another, bacteria can use their motility appendages, such as flagella, or hop a ride with other cells moving throughout our body (such as blood cells) by attaching to them.

Then, as bacteria colonize, migrate, and invade, they usually cause destruction to our cells and tissues. Sometimes this is an intended action, and other times it is a consequence of our own immune system acting on the pathogen. The reason a bacterial pathogen might want to intentionally destroy our cells is to gain access to underlying tissue during migration. To do this, bacteria produce specialized enzymes that can destroy our cells and break down **connective tissue**, biological material that binds organs and limbs. These enzymes help carve out a path for the bacteria to travel down during disease.

In many diseases, such as the ones discussed in this book, cell and tissue destruction is actually caused by the body itself. How does this happen? The immune system can be both a blessing and a curse. When a foreign antigen, such as a bacterial pathogen, infects a person, the immune system releases white blood cells and proteins called **cytokines**, which mediate the immune response. The release of cytokines results in a rush of immune cells to the site of infection and an increase in temperature, a process called **inflammation**. This is why an infection on our skin becomes red, raised, and hot (inflamed), and why fevers develop when we have an infection. The immune cells that rush to the infection site then produce destructive enzymes in an attempt to destroy the bacterial pathogen. However, these destructive enzymes often destroy our own cells too. Thus, although bacteria may not directly cause destruction, they can initiate and mediate the process.

Finally, a successful pathogen must not only survive and persist in the host, but it must also travel to and colonize other hosts. This process, called **dissemination**, results in the spread of bacteria throughout an environment or population. *M. tuberculosis* is a highly successful pathogen partly because of its ability to disseminate throughout the population. The mechanisms of dissemination vary for different bacterial pathogens depending on the part of the body they affect. For example, *Haemophilus influenzae* (the cause of ear and respiratory infections) and *Streptococcus pyogenes* (the cause of strep throat) live in the respiratory tract (throat, lungs) and are disseminated when you cough or sneeze. In contrast, *Vibrio cholerae* (the cause of cholera) colonizes the digestive tract and is spread through feces. Like the organisms we discuss here, coughing and sharing toothbrushes are ways oral bacteria are spread from one individual to another.

The general life cycle of a bacterial pathogen has just been described. As bacteria travel through our bodies and jump from host to host, they are constantly being attacked by our own immune system. In most cases, the immune system wins. However, sometimes the bacteria win, and humans develop symptoms of disease and have to take medication, such as antibiotics. The reason the immune system is not always able to eliminate the pathogen is that bacteria have developed very intricate ways of evading the immune response. The interaction between the host and pathogen can be thought of as a battle, where sometimes humans have the sword and the bacterium holds the shield, and other times the bacterium holds the sword and humans defend with a shield.

The number of tools that bacteria employ for evading the immune system is great, but perhaps the best studied of the bacterial tools is bacterial toxins. A bacterial toxin is a protein that either kills or disrupts the normal functions of host cells. Some toxins, such as **hemolysin** and **leukotoxin** (also called leukocidin) destroy blood cells that are part of the immune system. Other toxins, such as anthrax and tetanus, take control of normal cells and impair their function.

STUDYING BACTERIA IN THE LABORATORY

To understand how bacteria cause disease and how we can effectively treat the disease, it is necessary to remove a bacterial pathogen from its natural environment and study it under the controlled conditions of a research laboratory. There are many tools that **microbiologists** use to study bacteria, and we will discuss several of them here.

THE MICROSCOPE

In the late 1600s, Antony van Leeuwenhoek in the Netherlands and Robert Hooke in England designed some of the first microscopes that were strong enough to magnify microorganisms (as much as 200 times). For his own entertainment Van Leeuwenhoek obtained plaque from his friends' teeth and examined the samples under his homemade microscopes. The drawings left behind from Van Leeuwenhoek show bacteria that he called "animalcules." In fact, his drawings were so detailed and accurate that some of the bacteria he depicted as seen swimming under his single-lens microscope more than 300 years ago can be recognized among bacteria today.

Today, the primary way microbiologists view bacteria is still through the use of a microscope. While the technology is much more advanced than Van Leeuwenhoek's homemade microscope, the principles of microscopy are the same—using light and lenses to magnify an object. There

WHAT MICROBIOLOGISTS DO

A microbiologist is someone who studies organisms that are too small to be seen with the naked eye. Microorganisms include bacteria, fungi, viruses, and protozoans. Some microbiologists, called industrial microbiologists, work at water treatment plants where they test the water to be sure it's free of dangerous microorganisms. Environmental microbiologists help keep our environment clean by using beneficial microorganisms to remove contaminated waste. Clinical microbiologists can be found working in hospitals where they have the important job of identifying bacteria that cause disease in patients. Research microbiologists work at universities and pharmaceutical companies where they study how microorganisms cause disease and ways to treat such diseases.

are two main types of microscopes: the light microscope and electron microscope.

Most students learn to use the light microscope while in school. The light microscope has several main parts: illumination source, condenser, stage, objective lenses, and eyepieces. The illumination source of a standard light microscope is a lightbulb that emits photons (just like standard lightbulbs). As the photons leave the bulb, they must be directed and focused onto the specimen that is mounted on a glass slide. This is the job of the glass condenser lens, which is located just below the specimen stage. The photons then pass through the glass slide and specimen, which is located on the stage, and into the objective lenses. The glass objective lenses capture the light passing through the specimen and magnify the image. Finally, the eyepiece lenses that you look through further magnify the image. The total magnification of the specimen can be calculated by multiplying the magnification power of the objective lens by the power of the eyepiece lens. A typical light microscope has objective lenses of 10x, 40x, or 100x with an eyepiece magnification of 10x. Therefore, a specimen viewed with a 10x eyepiece and 40x objective lens would be magnified 400x.

The most important property of a microscope is not magnification but **resolution**. Resolution is defined as the smallest distance between two objects where the two objects are still distinguishable. Let's use your own eyes to demonstrate resolution. Use your pen or pencil to draw two dots about 3 inches (7.6 centimeters) apart from each other. Lean the paper upright and step back a few feet. You can clearly see that there appear to be two dots and not one. Now take your pencil and sharpen it really well or use a fine-point pen to draw two more dots essentially next to each other, as close as possible. Lean the paper up again and step back the same distance as before. It is probably very difficult for you to determine whether there is one dot or more (this may work better with a friend who does not see you draw two dots). When you can no longer see two separate dots, the distance between the two dots is the limit of resolution. For

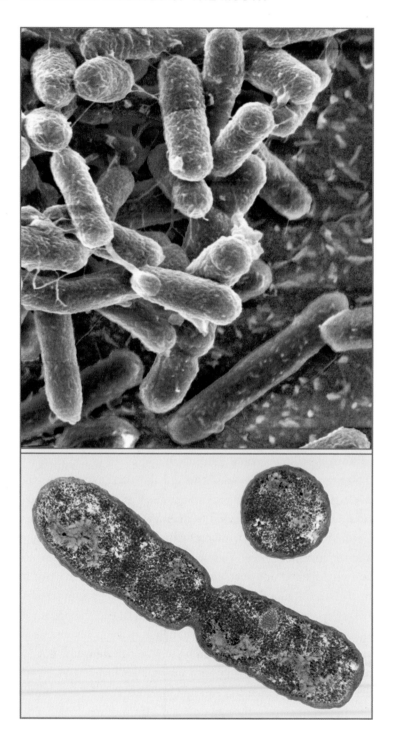

a light microscope, the resolution limit is approximately 0.2 μm (a micrometer is one-millionth of a meter).

The more powerful electron microscopes can be found in research laboratories and universities (Figure 2.6). The principles of an electron microscope are similar to those of the light microscope, except that the illumination source of an electron microscope is electrons instead of photons, and the lenses are essentially magnets rather than glass. Because electrons have a much smaller wavelength (greater energy) than photons, the resolution of electron microscopes is better than for light microscopes (about 100 times better.). There are two main types of electron microscopes: the scanning electron microscope and the transmission electron microscope. The microscopes differ in the way they make an image of a specimen and the type of image they generate. In the scanning electron microscope, the electrons "scan" across a specimen and record the topological features of it. The result is a three-dimensional image of the specimen. In the transmission electron microscope, the electrons are "transmitted" through the specimen. The result is a two-dimensional image of the specimen that can reveal its internal features.

GROWING BACTERIA

To thoroughly study a bacterium, it is necessary not only to visualize it but also to grow it in the laboratory, a process called **culturing**. Just as each type of animal feeds on different foods, bacteria have specific nutritional requirements. Some of the common types of **growth media** that bacteria use as a food source include yeast extract, beef broth, brain and heart extract, and glucose. In addition to nutritional requirements,

Figure 2.6 *(opposite page)* This figure shows the different types of images that a scanning (top) and transmission (bottom) electron microscope acquire. (Gary Gauglen/Dr. Dennis Kunkel/Visuals Unlimited)

bacteria also have environmental requirements, including temperature, oxygen levels, and light intensity. For example, some bacteria can grow only under **anaerobic** (no oxygen) conditions while others require oxygen for growth (**aerobic**). For bacteria to grow best, they must be **incubated** under their optimal nutritional and environmental conditions.

Bacteria are typically grown two different ways: on semisolid media in petri dishes and in liquid broth. The difference between the semisolid and liquid formats is that the semisolid media contains **agar**. Agar is a gelling agent that melts at boiling temperatures and then solidifies as it cools (just like gelatin). Agar is actually purified from seaweed and is even used in ice cream to keep it soft.

When bacteria grow on semisolid media, they form **colonies**. A colony arises from a single cell that is placed on the medium and then divides numerous times. When enough cells accumulate in that spot (hundreds of millions), a colony forms. All cells within a colony are just like each other. The purpose of growing bacteria on a semisolid medium is to isolate and identify an individual type of bacterium.

After a microbiologist is able to isolate the bacterium of interest, it is cultured in liquid broth containing nutrients for the bacteria to utilize. In liquid broth, the bacteria grow in suspension rather than in one place as they do on semisolid media. As bacteria grow in liquid broth, they reduce the clarity of the liquid and turn it cloudy, or turbid, just like water sitting in a flower vase after many days. Greater turbidity is indicative of a greater number of individual bacterial cells in the broth. Some bacteria grow so well that after only 24 hours of incubation, the liquid can be filled with more than one billion cells per milliliter!

SEQUENCING BACTERIAL DNA

In 1977, Frederick Sanger and colleagues developed a method for determining the nucleotide sequence of a piece of DNA. Nearly 30 years later, a modern variation of the Sanger method is still used for sequencing DNA. DNA sequencing allows scientists to determine which genes an organism contains and the types of mutations that result in a certain property, and to design drugs that can target genes for antimicrobial therapy.

In 1995, *Haemophilus influenzae* became the first bacterium to have its **genome** fully sequenced. The project took several years to complete. With greater technology and increased automation, it is now possible to sequence bacterial genomes in a matter of weeks. To date, more than 230 bacterial genomes have been fully sequenced with more being completed all the time.

3

The Mouth–
A Bacterium's
Dream Home

The mouth is a breeding ground for bacteria. It's warm and moist, accessible, rich in nutrients, and has many surfaces to bind to. As we discussed in the second chapter, sometimes bacteria can penetrate deeper into tissues of the mouth, and this can cause disease. In this chapter, we will examine the architecture and elevation of the oral cavity and reveal the multitude of places pathogenic bacteria can be found and cause disease.

THE MOUTH

The Greek philosopher Aristotle believed that men had more teeth than women and that one's teeth grow throughout a person's lifetime. We now know that both of these ideas are false. There is no correlation between number of teeth and gender. In addition, your teeth do not continue growing once they have fully formed. You get 20 baby teeth and a maximum of 32 adult teeth, and that's it. In contrast to a young child, if you lose a tooth, you don't grow it back. This is why it's so important to take care of your teeth and have good oral health. Visiting your dentist regularly helps you accomplish this goal.

The most prominent part of the oral cavity is the teeth, but the oral cavity also includes buccal surfaces (inside of cheeks), the tongue, salivary glands, saliva, and plaque, to name a few. We'll begin our anatomical discussion of the mouth with the teeth.

What is the function of teeth? Most people would say "to chew food." But teeth serve many other functions, including providing support for other structures in the mouth, aiding in swallowing and digestion, helping us speak and pronounce words correctly, and contributing to our appearance. The emotional stress that poor oral appearance (such as missing or stained teeth) can have on a child or adolescent is significant.

Each tooth has a distinctive shape. The teeth in the back of the mouth have flat broad surfaces while those in the front are more narrow and sharp. Each tooth performs a specific function that is highly specialized. Let's begin at the back of the mouth and work forward (Figure 3.1). The back teeth are called the molars. The molars are good at chewing and grinding food before the food is allowed to pass down the esophagus and into your stomach. Adults have a maximum of 12 molars. The rear-most molars are also called wisdom teeth. In front of the molars are the bicuspids or premolars. The bicuspids crush and tear food. In front of the bicuspids are the cuspids or canines. The cuspids have pointed tops that help us hold and

ABOUT DENTISTS

Just as a cardiologist is a heart specialist, a dentist is a specialist of the mouth. Dentists treat infections in the mouth, diagnose and treat oral cancer and oral genetic diseases, perform surgery to remove teeth and treat disease, and help us keep a bright, healthy smile. A dentist has many years of education and training. After four years of college, one must then attend dental school (there are 55 dental schools in the United States) for four more years. For specialization (such as orthodontics or periodontology), two or three more years of training are required. Although time-intensive, a career as a dentist can be exciting and rewarding, knowing that you are helping your patients.

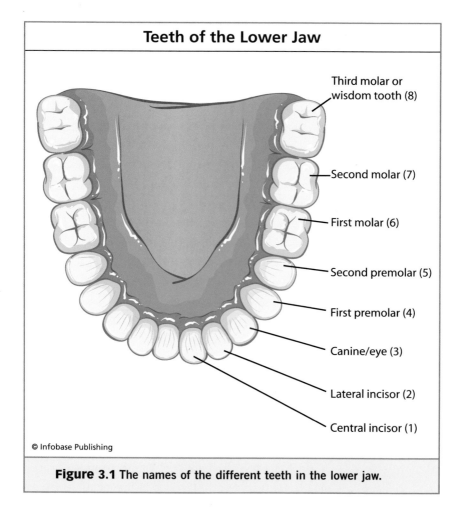

Teeth of the Lower Jaw

Third molar or wisdom tooth (8)

Second molar (7)

First molar (6)

Second premolar (5)

First premolar (4)

Canine/eye (3)

Lateral incisor (2)

Central incisor (1)

© Infobase Publishing

Figure 3.1 The names of the different teeth in the lower jaw.

tear food. Finally, the sharp teeth in the front of the mouth are called incisors. The incisors have biting edges that cut food.

As we discuss infectious diseases of the teeth, you will see that some diseases affect certain teeth and not others. Think about the shape and location of certain teeth to see if you can figure out why diseases may be **localized**.

The teeth are the hardest structures in the body and can be divided into two parts: the **crown** and the **root** (Figure 3.2). The visible part of our tooth is called the crown. The root extends below the gum line. The outermost layer of the crown is composed of **enamel**. Enamel is a calcium-containing substance that protects the inside of the tooth from harmful bacteria and allows the tooth to withstand the pressures of biting and eating. Below the enamel is **dentin**. The dentin also contains calcium and is about as hard as bone. Dentin protects the **pulp**, the living tissue of the tooth. Pulp is composed of blood vessels, which provide the necessary nourishment to the interior of the tooth, and nerve and connective tissue. The part of the pulp that is in the crown of the tooth is called the pulp chamber and the part that is in the root is called the root canal. Attached to the dentin in the root of the tooth is the **cementum**. The cementum "cements" or anchors the tooth into the jawbone. The cementum is also as hard as bone.

The tissue surrounding the teeth is called the **periodontium**. The periodontium is made up of four parts: the **gingiva**, the cementum, the **periodontal ligament**, and the **alveolar process** (Figure 3.2). The gingiva is the tissue surrounding the teeth, also known as the gums. The periodontal ligament holds the tooth in place by connecting the cementum to the alveolar process, a bony structure that is the anchor plate for the periodontal ligament and provides stabilization for our teeth.

The infectious diseases we will discuss in this book are localized predominantly to the teeth and the periodontium. However, the tongue and buccal surfaces also play important roles in disease by acting as reservoirs for bacteria, as some pathogens "hang out" on the tongue and buccal surfaces. If you've ever looked at your cheek scrapings under a microscope, you will notice many tiny cells attaching to a gigantic one. That's bacteria attached to your cheek cells (see Figure 2.1).

Other important organs within the mouth that can affect disease outcome include the **salivary glands**. The salivary glands produce and secrete **saliva**. Three pairs of major salivary glands and many minor ones produce saliva. Saliva production is an involuntary action, just like breathing and heart beating. Saliva plays multiple roles, including aiding in food digestion, eliminating harmful microorganisms, providing lubrication

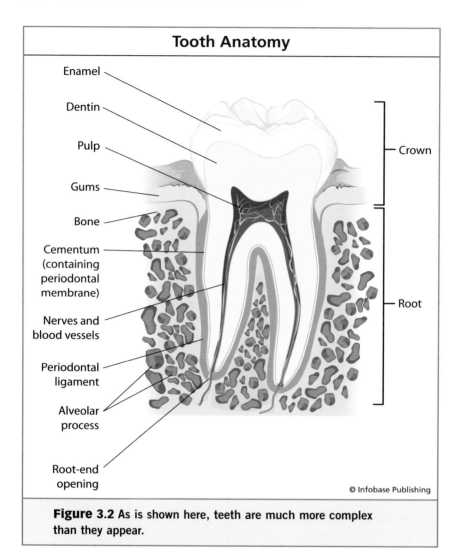

Tooth Anatomy

Enamel

Dentin

Pulp

Gums

Bone

Cementum
(containing
periodontal
membrane)

Nerves and
blood vessels

Periodontal
ligament

Alveolar
process

Root-end
opening

Crown

Root

© Infobase Publishing

Figure 3.2 As is shown here, teeth are much more complex than they appear.

during chewing, and providing a fluid environment for important enzymatic reactions to take place in.

For helping us digest foods, saliva contains an enzyme called amylase. Amylase breaks down starch, a major component in most of the foods we eat. Amylase helps break down our food into smaller, softer pieces before it enters our digestive tract.

Saliva may provide bacteria with a warm and moist environment, but saliva can also be toxic to bacteria. Saliva contains an enzyme called lysozyme. Lysozyme is able to destroy the cell walls of bacteria, effectively killing them. Saliva also contains histatin, a peptide that can kill pathogenic bacteria and fungi. Perhaps the most potent antimicrobial component of saliva is **salivary antibody**. Antibodies are proteins that our bodies produce to combat pathogens. Antibodies bind to pathogens and "label" them as foreign so that other cells, such as **phagocytes**, can come and eliminate them from the body. Lysozyme and histatin have general killing properties, but antibodies target specific microorganisms.

If it weren't for saliva, we would always have dry mouths, making for a very dangerous situation (**xerostomia** is a condition of dry mouth). Within saliva are large proteins called **mucins** that give saliva its hydrating ability. Recent research has shown that mucins also help protect us from acid reflux disease by acting as a natural buffer.

MICROBIOLOGY OF THE MOUTH

The human mouth contains more than 500 species of bacteria. Luckily, most of the bacteria in our mouths are beneficial bacteria, not pathogens. These beneficial bacteria constitute the **normal flora**. In fact, it is the normal flora that keeps us healthy by excluding foreign pathogens by leaving them few places to go. The immune system also helps prevent oral disease. With 500 types of bacteria inhabiting the mouth, where can they all live? The answer is **plaque**. Everyone has seen or felt tooth plaque, especially when they haven't brushed their teeth in a while (Figure 3.3). Plaque is a mass of bacteria and their synthesized products (such as proteins and polysaccharide) adhering to the surface of teeth. The cells in plaque are so numerous that in one gram (.04 ounces) of dental plaque, there are approximately 100 billion bacterial cells. Plaque is a perfect example of a biofilm.

Plaque undergoes a developmental process just as our own body does. The end result is a highly organized and evolved structure that humans will never be able to eliminate. The first bacterium that usually initiates plaque formation is known as *Streptococcus mutans*. As we will learn in a later chapter, this bacterium plays a key role in the development of cavities. Over time, other bacteria colonize and make their way into plaque, with each species making an important contribution to the formation and maintenance of the plaque biofilm.

The easiest way to study plaque bacteria is to culture them in the laboratory as described in the previous chapter. Scientists have been able to culture only about one-half of the species in the mouth because we have not yet figured out the types of nutrients these bacteria require for growth. That means that the other half, although we know they are there from other techniques, have never before been grown outside

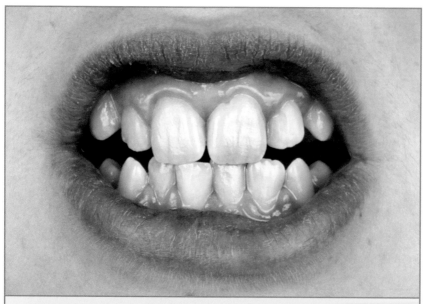

Figure 3.3 Plaque is indicated here in blue, after this teenager chewed on a tablet designed to help locate plaque. (Alex Bartel/ Photo Researchers, Inc.)

RESEARCH FUNDING

Research costs money. If it were not for research that has been done in oral health, most of us would probably not maintain a full set of teeth for very long. A large part of the oral health research funding in the United States comes from the National Institute of Dental and Craniofacial Research (NIDCR), established in 1948. The NIDCR generously supports research and education in the oral health sciences and their money comes from taxpayers. During fiscal year 2005, NIDCR contributed $389.4 million in grants to support research and education.

of the mouth. There is a great need for oral biology researchers to conduct further study of oral bacteria.

THE MOUTH IS CONNECTED TO THE BODY

The mouth is a pathogen's door to the rest of the body. Taking care of one's teeth doesn't just mean better oral health. It means better overall health. In recent years it has become increasingly clear that individuals with poor oral health are at higher risk for diseases such as heart disease. For example, bacteria that cause certain types of endocarditis (inflammation of heart valves) are also found in our oral cavity.

4

Gingivitis

Gingivitis (also referred to as gum disease) is inflammation of the gingiva, or gums (Figure 4.1). In gingivitis, the damage that occurs can be reversed and there is no permanent loss of supporting structures of the teeth (however, gingivitis can progress to periodontal disease—a highly destructive disease, discussed in the next chapter). Gingivitis is characterized by swelling and reddening of the gum tissue. The tissue becomes very sensitive and bleeds easily during brushing. Surprisingly, gingivitis usually does not cause pain. This can be both a blessing and a curse. Although no one wants to be in pain, pain is a signal from our bodies that something is wrong. When we feel pain, we immediately act to alleviate the pain or to find the cause of it. If something is wrong, such as in gingivitis, and the problem is not addressed, it can become worse and possibly irreversible. Chances are, either you or the person sitting next to you will have gingivitis within your lifetimes. Gingivitis affects more than half the population and the prevalence becomes even greater as we age. Perhaps you could help decrease this number within your lifetime by learning more about gingivitis and the simple ways to prevent it.

How do you know if you will get gingivitis? There is really no way to tell for sure. Even if you do everything right (brush your teeth, visit the dentist, etc.), you may still get the disease.

Why is that? There are many uncontrollable factors that can affect your chances of contracting the disease and the severity of the disease. For example, pregnant women are more prone to getting gingivitis, as are individuals of African-American and Mexican descents compared with other ethnic groups. Men have a higher incidence of gingivitis than do women.

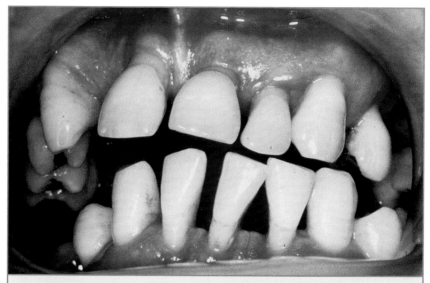

Figure 4.1 This person has severe gingivitis. Certain teeth have less tissue surrounding them than others. (Biophoto Associates/ Photo Researchers, Inc.)

MICROBIOLOGY OF DISEASE

You may be waiting to learn about which bacterium causes gingivitis. Unfortunately there is no individual organism that is responsible for the disease. Unlike cholera or anthrax (which are caused by *Vibrio cholerae* and *Bacillus anthracis*, respectively), gingivitis is the result of many types of bacteria colonizing the oral cavity. Some of the bacteria commonly associated with gingivitis include *Streptococcus sp.*, *Actinomyces sp.*, *Capnocytophaga sp.*, *Fusobacterium sp.*, *Prevotella sp.*, *Campylobacter gracilis*, *Peptostreptococcus micros*, *Eubacterium nodatum*, *Campylobacter concisus*, and *Eikenella corrodens*. These bacteria are all part of plaque.

Bacteria alone, however, are not enough to cause disease. Gingivitis is a disease that requires both plaque bacteria and our immune response. Very simply, gingivitis is the result of our immune system responding to abnormal plaque accumulation on the tooth surface. The outcome is an inflammatory response in the gum tissue (hence redness and swelling). When we maintain proper oral care, our plaque remains at minimal, healthy levels. When we stop brushing or don't see a dentist regularly, plaque accumulation occurs and our body develops an immune response against the "foreign invaders."

What type of immune response does our body mount? Several components of the immune response are activated during gingivitis. First, an immediate response occurs that results in the migration of inflammatory cells to the gingiva. These cells produce cytokines. Some of these cytokines cause our blood vessels to dilate (become more porous and leaky) within the area of infection (the gingivae in this case). This causes leakage of blood cells in the gingiva, which results in the redness and swelling that is characteristic of gingivitis. Cytokines also tell certain cells to produce destructive proteins that help destroy bacterial cells. The problem is, in addition to killing bacteria, the destructive proteins also damage our own cells and cause tissue breakdown (Figure 4.2).

THE EVOLUTION OF THE TOOTHBRUSH

Talk about hard bristles: The earliest toothbrushes were made by chewing on twigs and tree roots until the plant fibers formed a "brush." Several thousand years later, in the 1600s, the Greeks learned to use a rough towel to wipe their teeth every morning. Finally, in 1780, the English developed the first modern toothbrush, which had a handle made of bone and animal hair for bristles. The toothbrush was first patented in the United States in 1857, with polished cattle thigh bones forming an excellent toothbrush handle. Through the years, the toothbrush has gone through many makeovers, but its purpose has remained the same: to keep our teeth clean and healthy.

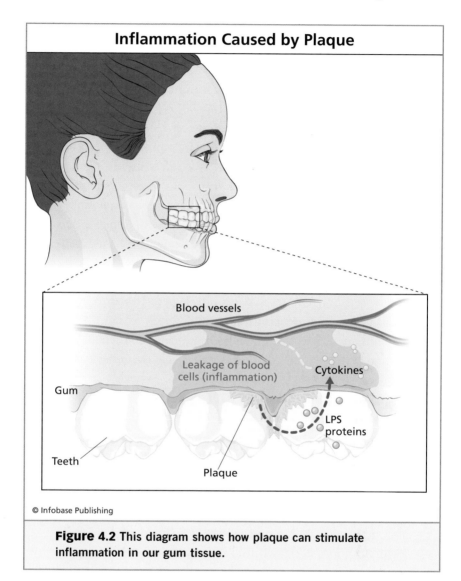

Inflammation Caused by Plaque

Blood vessels

Leakage of blood cells (inflammation)

Cytokines

Gum

LPS proteins

Teeth

Plaque

© Infobase Publishing

Figure 4.2 This diagram shows how plaque can stimulate inflammation in our gum tissue.

A second, more delayed response is the production of antibodies. This process takes longer than the production of cytokines because several cell types, B-cells and T-cells, must process and "analyze" all the bacterial proteins before an antibody is actually produced. Once antibodies are produced, which takes several days, our immune system begins to target and eliminate the foreign bacteria and proteins. In the process of eliminating plaque bacteria, bacterial guts are released, including LPS, DNA, and intracellular proteins. These bacterial components further stimulate the immune system as described above for the immediate response.

To put all this simply, gingivitis is really no different from getting an infection on your skin, which also becomes swollen, red, and sensitive due to the immune response to the microorganisms.

You may be asking yourself, "Why does a large amount of plaque cause an inflammatory response?" Excess plaque means lots of bacteria and their bioproducts. Remember from Chapter 2, Gram-negative bacteria produce LPS. LPS is highly reactive with the immune system and the large amount of LPS in plaque sets our immune systems into hyperactive mode. Bacteria also contain numerous kinds of different proteins. These proteins are different from our own proteins and therefore are foreign to our bodies. Our bodies want to get rid of the foreign proteins, so antibodies are produced.

When the immune system is not working properly, bacteria grow uncontrollably and disease can become worse. Our immune system can be adversely affected (**immuno-compromised**) by diseases (such as in AIDS) or by environmental factors. Not surprisingly, smoking is one environmental factor that plays a role in a large percentage of gingivitis cases in the United States. Additionally, smokers experience more severe disease when they get gingivitis than nonsmokers do. The toxic products in cigarettes cause decreased wound healing, reduced ability for immune cells to eliminate pathogens, and a reduction in the connective tissue that makes up the gingivae.

So far we've discussed bacterial bioproducts that act indirectly by causing our immune system to produce damaging products. But bacteria can also directly damage tissue. Some bacteria produce toxins that kill connective tissue and cells. Certain bacterial proteins can even destroy antibodies and cells of our immune system.

PREVENTION AND TREATMENT

You probably already know the best way to prevent gingivitis: by brushing and flossing, using mouthwash, and visiting your dentist regularly. Because gingivitis is reversible, the best way to prevent and treat the disease is to improve your oral hygiene. When someone has gingivitis, there are three possible outcomes. If they restore or improve their oral health, gingivitis is eliminated. If they continue what they are doing, gingivitis may become **persistent** and remain the same indefinitely. Or, gingivitis may get worse and result in a more serious disease, periodontitis, which we will discuss in the next chapter.

Treatment for gingivitis focuses on eliminating plaque and the factors that promote it. Removing plaque means brushing and flossing correctly. When you visit your dentist, he or she will examine and clean your teeth using different types of instruments (see Figure 5.4). These instruments are able to remove plaque in places you may not be able to reach with your toothbrush.

STUDIES IN GINGIVITIS RESEARCH

How would you like it if you came to school one day and your science teacher told you that for an experiment, you couldn't brush or floss your teeth or use mouthwash? This is exactly what dental researchers do to study gingivitis. In the 1960s, a group of scientists first performed this experiment, and it is still being used today. During the experiment, volunteers are asked not to brush, floss, or use mouthwash for three weeks. Can you predict what happens on their teeth? That's right, a huge amount of plaque builds up and the now hygienically challenged volunteers get gingivitis. Why do researchers want to do this? Causing gingivitis in humans allows researchers to study which factors may contribute to gingivitis. For example, researchers have used smokers and nonsmokers in studies to see if smoking affects the disease. They also look at differences in gingivitis progression (how long it takes for the disease to occur) and severity (how bad the disease is) in males and females. Researchers can also try new types of treatments to determine which ones are best at resolving gingivitis. At the end of the experiment, the volunteers are allowed to brush, floss, and use mouthwash to restore their good oral health.

5

Periodontal Disease

In Chapter 4, we learned about inflammation of the gums, gingivitis. When gingivitis becomes worse, it can proceed to periodontal disease. Periodontal disease is irreversible and involves destruction of the structures that hold our teeth in place. These structures include the periodontal ligament and the alveolar bone (see Figure 3.2). The destruction is caused by a specific microorganism or groups of microorganisms.

The periodontal ligament is made of **collagen** and connects the root of the tooth to the alveolar bone, as noted in Chapter 3. Collagen is a protein that makes up much of the connective tissue in the body. In the periodontal ligament, collagen is arranged in bundles (Figure 5.1). These bundles give the ligament its great strength and ability to hold our teeth in place. The periodontal ligament also contains cells and vessels that help supply nutrients to the gingiva and surrounding region. In addition, the periodontal ligament is supplied with nerves that allow us to feel pressure and pain when we bite down or have a tooth pulled.

The key feature of periodontal disease is that there is loss of attachment between the tooth and the gingiva (Figure 5.2). The destruction of the periodontal ligament and alveolar bone causes a "pocket"; a dentist can measure the depth of a pocket in a process called periodontal probing. The amount of bone loss determines the severity of disease, with two to three millimeters (.08–.12 inches) indicating mild disease and five millimeters (.20 in.) or more indicating severe disease.

There are several forms of periodontal disease, the two most common being chronic periodontitis (formerly known as adult periodontitis) and aggressive periodontitis (formerly known as juvenile periodontitis). The three main differences between these forms of

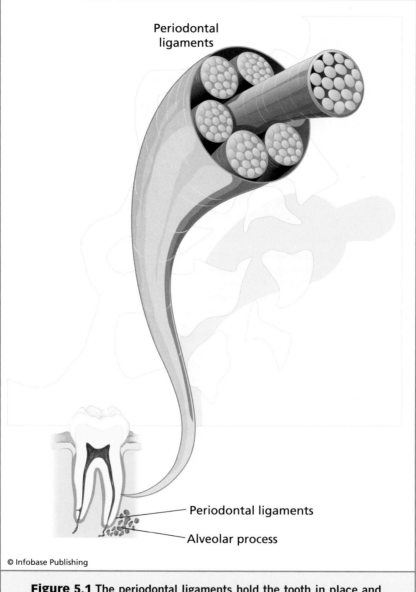

Periodontal
ligaments

Periodontal ligaments

Alveolar process

© Infobase Publishing

Figure 5.1 The periodontal ligaments hold the tooth in place and are made of strong collagen fibers that are assembled like cables.

the disease are 1) the speed at which they progress; 2) the population groups they affect; and 3) the types of bacteria that cause them.

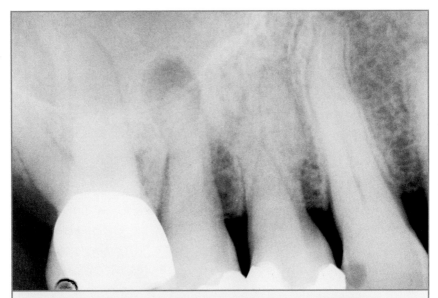

Figure 5.2 This x-ray image shows periodontal disease. Bone loss is visible as the darkened areas next to the three teeth on the right. The second tooth from the left shows a periapical cyst with a large abscess at its root. (Phototake, Inc.)

Chronic periodontitis occurs in individuals older than 35 years and progresses at a relatively slow rate. Chronic periodontitis affects more than half of the adult population; not surprisingly, cigarette smoking significantly increases your risk of getting the disease.

In aggressive periodontitis, the disease progresses rapidly. Within months, tooth loss can occur if treatment isn't sought. The disease occurs most often in adolescents and affects certain ethnic groups more than others. People who get aggressive periodontitis often have a genetic predisposition for the disease, which means the disease runs in their family.

MICROBIOLOGY OF DISEASE

Like gingivitis, periodontal disease is initiated by bacteria, but our own bodies' response also plays an important role. The bacteria that accumulate in plaque cause a response by our immune system. This response can be both helpful and harmful. The formation of the periodontal pocket is a key step to periodontal disease progression, since plaque can accumulate in the pocket. This pocket full of plaque is very difficult to remove because of its hidden location. As bacteria accumulate in the pocket, so do the destructive products of the bacteria and our own immune response. These products ultimately destroy cells in the periodontal pocket, enhancing disease.

CHRONIC PERIODONTITIS

Chronic periodontitis is believed to be caused by several different bacteria, but the most commonly associated ones are: *Tannerella forsythia, Fusobacterium nucleatum, Treponema denticola,* and *Porphyromonas gingivalis.* Usually two or more bacterial species interact with each other to cause chronic periodontal disease. This is called a **polymicrobial infection**. Think about how a self-sustaining farm works. Each worker has a specific job to carry out, and when everyone does his or her part, an effective community exists. The same is true for a polymicrobial infection.

THE FORSYTH INSTITUTE

The Forsyth Institute was founded in 1910 by Thomas, John, and Mary Forsyth in honor of their father, James Bennett Forsyth, who had a dream of founding a dental clinic for the children of Boston. Over the years, The Forsyth Institute has made significant discoveries in the field of dental research. In the 1960s, researchers at Forsyth discovered that a bacterium, *Streptococcus mutans*, causes dental decay and cavities. They also studied the role of fluoride in preventing cavities. In 1993, the institute began an Educational Outreach program to provide internships for high school students interested in dental research. Information about this outreach program can be found at: http://www.forsyth.org/forsyth.asp?pg=100068.

Each bacterium lends something unique that creates the right environment for it to cause disease.

Tannerella forsythensis

This bacterium is Gram negative and is anaerobic, which means that it does not like oxygen. In fact, when growing the bacterium in a lab, it will not grow unless you remove all the oxygen from its environment. The bacterium is rod-shaped and variable in size. The genus name *Tannerella* is derived from the person who first identified the bacterium in periodontal tissue, Dr. Anne Tanner. The species name, *forsythensis*, came from the Forsyth Institute, where Dr. Tanner isolated this bacterium.

This bacterium contributes to disease with destruction-causing enzymes such as proteases and **sialidase**. These enzymes are able to break up our own proteins and carbohydrates, causing local tissue destruction, which makes disease worse.

Fusobacterium nucleatum

The Latin term "fusus" means *spindle*. Can you think of the shape of this bacterium? If you guessed that it's a pointed shape, you're correct (Figure 5.3). The genus, *Fusobacterium*, was identified in 1922 by a German scientist, as he described pointed Gram-negative bacilli found in the mouth. The species name, *nucleatum*, describes the nucleated (spherical in shape) appearance of structures within the bacterium under the microscope. The appearance is due to granules within the cytosol of the cell.

This bacterium's claim to fame is that it is able to act as a bridge, binding to many types of bacteria and "bridging together" bacteria that can bind directly to the tooth surface with those that cannot. An analogy would be using glue to bind two sheets of paper. Without the glue, the papers won't stick to each other. *F. nucleatum* acts as the glue between different types of bacteria. What does the bacterium produce that allows it to interact with so many types of bacteria? *F. nucleatum* has special structures (called **lectins**) on its

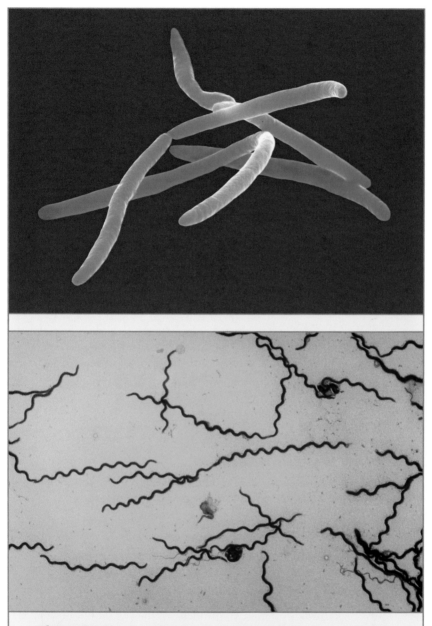

Figure 5.3 Shown in this figure are some of the types of bacteria that can cause periodontal disease. On the top is *Fusobacterium nucleatum*, and on the bottom is *Treponema denticola*.
(Dr. Dennis Kunkel/Dr. T.J. Beveridge/Visuals Unlimited)

outer membrane that can bind polysaccharides of other bacteria. Scientists also use lectins as research tools to study polysaccharides of biological importance.

Treponema denticola

This bacterium is a treponeme, or spirochete, which means it is spiral-shaped (Figure 5.3). Because of this shape, it is easy to identify in drawings and pictures. In fact, we know that nearly 350 years ago, Antony van Leeuwenhoek observed these bacteria from the teeth scrapings he sampled under his famous microscopes. Like *T. forsythia* and *F. nucleatum*, this bacterium is also Gram negative and anaerobic.

T. denticola produces many different products that lead to periodontal disease. Like *T. forsythia*, this bacterium also produces many proteases that can destroy tissue. In addition, *T. denticola* can bind directly to red blood cells (called **hemagglutination**) and can even destroy them (called **hemolysis**). As discussed previously, this bacterium also causes immune cells to produce enzymes that can cause tissue breakdown. The most famous of these enzymes is called **collagenase**, which destroys collagen, the substance of the periodontal ligament.

Porphyromonas gingivalis

This bacterium is perhaps the best studied of all periodontal pathogens. The genus *Porphyromonas* means "black pigmented" and refers to the color of the colonies that form on agar. The species name *gingivalis* refers to where it is found, in the gingiva. The number of factors that *P. gingivalis* produces in order to cause disease is immense.

P. gingivalis is able to bind to many different cell types in the mouth using its pili. Once attached to the cells, the bacteria can enter them (using invasins) and actually survive and grow inside. From the inside of a cell, *P. gingivalis* can hide from the immune system and alter the functions of the cell. Thus, our own cells actually become the headquarters for *P. gingivalis*.

P. gingivalis also produces proteases called gingipains. Like the other Gram-negative bacteria, the LPS of *P. gingivalis* plays an important role in periodontal disease.

AGGRESSIVE PERIODONTITIS

This disease is similar to the chronic form of the disease, except that aggressive periodontitis worsens more rapidly and the causative agent is primarily one bacterium, *Actinobacillus actinomycetemcomitans*. Because the name of the bacterium is so long, it is often abbreviated *Aa*. As mentioned in Chapter 2, *Actinobacillus* refers to the rod shape of the bacterium. The species name *actinomycetemcomitans* means "found with *Actinomyces*." *Aa* was originally identified in oral lesions with the Gram-positive bacterium *Actinomyces sp.*

Aa is a Gram-negative bacterium that is not completely anaerobic but actually prefers an environment enriched with carbon dioxide. One of the most interesting properties of this bacterium is its ability to attach to so many surfaces. In fact, this is one of the best biofilm-forming bacteria known. Its ability to attach helps the bacterium colonize teeth and other cells in the mouth. Increased colonization means a greater ability to cause disease. Another factor that helps this bacterium cause periodontal disease is a toxin called leukotoxin. Leukotoxin kills white blood cells (leukocytes), which helps it avoid the immune system.

In summary, bacteria have many different components that contribute to disease. In many cases, more than one bacterium may possess similar tools to cause disease (such as LPS and proteases). In other cases, a bacterium may have something unusual about it.

PREVENTION AND TREATMENT

Because periodontal disease is irreversible, simple brushing and flossing will not eliminate the disease once you have it. Instead, a person with periodontal disease usually has to visit a periodontist, a dentist whose specialty is treating periodontal

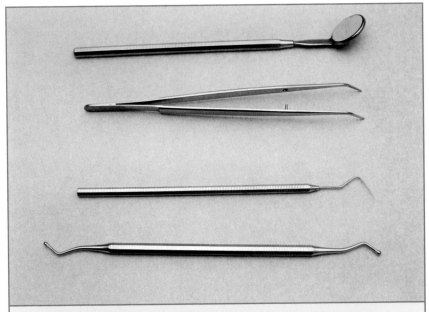

Figure 5.4 Tools of the dentist. Shown here from top to bottom are a mirror, tweezers, a probe, and curettes. All of these tools are used to examine or treat areas of the mouth that are usually difficult to reach with a regular toothbrush. (Ruediger Knobloch/ A.B./zefa/Corbis)

disease. The goal of periodontal treatment is to keep the tissues that surround the teeth healthy. Unhealthy tissue promotes the growth of bacteria and plaque, which further worsens the disease. **Periodontal debridement** is the process of removing plaque and its by-products. Periodontal debridement is carried out using hand instruments as well as an ultrasonic device.

The first step of treatment is determining that a person has periodontal disease, by measuring the depth of a periodontal pocket between the gingiva and the tooth. The measuring instrument that a periodontist uses is called a **probe** (Figure 5.4).

After determining that someone has the disease, treatment begins by cleaning the periodontal area. The hand instruments used to debride plaque are called **scalers** and **curettes** (Figure 5.4). These instruments are used to reach deep within narrow pockets. The way the periodontist holds the scalers and curettes determines the type of technique the dentist is using. Common techniques that are used are called scaling and root planing. In scaling, the periodontist "scales" down and across the teeth to remove plaque, while root planing involves scraping the teeth closer to the bottom, or root, of a tooth.

Ultrasonic scalers are power-driven devices that vibrate rapidly to fracture and dislodge plaque and deposits on tooth surfaces. An ultrasonic scaler has a fine tip to reach within the periodontal pocket. To remove the dead bacteria and plaque that is dislodged, water can be shot out the tip of the ultrasonic scaler. Think of an ultrasonic scaler as a miniature power washer for teeth.

Following periodontal debridement, it is often necessary to perform surgery. A periodontist is also a surgeon of the mouth. The periodontist performs surgery to reduce the deep pocket areas to ensure that a patient can reach and clean the area with a toothbrush. Surgery is also used for repairing tissue that may have been severely damaged due to disease.

The rule for periodontal patients is to regularly clean their teeth and surrounding gums. Periodontal patients must also visit their dentist and periodontist much more often than others (once every two to three months). Because the disease is irreversible, the constant cleaning and dental visits never end. To avoid lots of pain, surgeries, and trips to your friendly neighborhood dental professional, start practicing good oral hygiene now.

STUDIES IN PERIODONTAL RESEARCH

The field of periodontal research is progressing rapidly. Some of the most recent findings relate to genome sequencing and genetic engineering of the bacteria that cause disease.

In Chapter 2, we discussed DNA sequencing and how it can reveal the entire genetic code of an organism. To date, the genomes of all the bacteria discussed above that cause periodontal disease have been sequenced. This means that we can identify the genes and proteins contained within these bacteria. A bacterium contains thousands of different genes. Most of them we may never learn about because of limitations in hands-on research. However, with an exact DNA sequence of these genes, we not only know that they are there, but also we can perform experiments with them and determine if they play a role in disease.

Genetic engineering is a very useful way of studying bacteria. Using genetic engineering, scientists are creating "mutants" of these bacteria that no longer have certain genes. They can then study the defects of the mutants to determine what the functions of the missing genes are. For example, to study the role that pili play in disease, scientists would make a mutant *P. gingivalis* by removing the pilin gene from its chromosome and test this mutant for attachment to oral cells. They might find that this mutant can no longer attach to oral cells. They could thus conclude that pili are important for *P. gingivalis* to attach to oral cells and colonize. Scientists could then test whether the *P. gingivalis* pili mutant can attach to *Aa* bacterial cells. If they found that the mutant can still attach, they could conclude that pili are not required for *P. gingivalis* to attach to *Aa* cells.

With the new genetic tools that are being developed every day, it is now possible to perform genetic engineering experiments with even the most difficult to work with bacteria. This new research may someday lead to better treatments for periodontal disease.

6

Cavities

Cavities (also known as caries) are the most common childhood disease and most people, if not every person, reading this book has either had a cavity or will have a cavity within their lifetime. Visits to the dentist due to cavities are the number-one reason for children missing school, next to the common cold. Costs associated with this oral disease in the United States reach into the billions of dollars. Although most people know that sugar has something to do with causing cavities, there are many more pieces in the puzzle.

PATHOLOGY OF DISEASE

A cavity is exactly what the name means: an abnormal crevice on the surface of a tooth. A cavity can form on any tooth, but it commonly occurs on the molars in the back of the mouth (Figure 6.1 and 6.2). The tops of molars already have natural crevices that make a good starting point for bacteria. When food is chewed, it gets pushed from the front to the back of the mouth. Thus, small pieces of food can accumulate on the back teeth, which help feed the bacteria there.

Why are cavities bad? As we learned in previous chapters, bacteria love to hide out in protected environments where our toothbrushes and saliva cannot easily reach. Within a cavity, bacteria can remain for a long period of time and cause further disease. As bacteria accumulate in the cavity, they can drill their way to the pulp of the tooth, resulting in **endodontic infections**. Endodontic infections are much more serious than cavities and require surgery for treatment, which will be discussed in the next chapter.

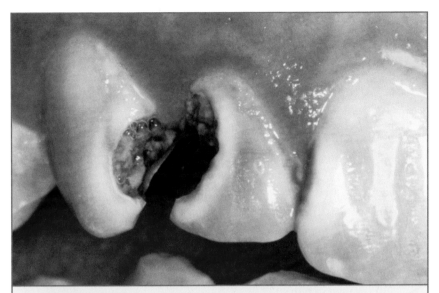

Figure 6.1 Human teeth with severe cavities. (Biophoto Associates/Photo Researchers, Inc.)

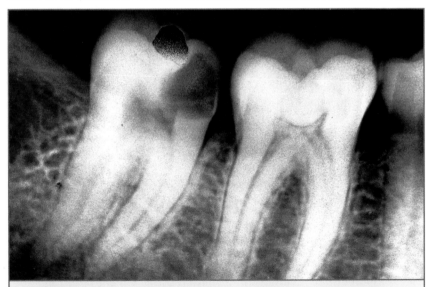

Figure 6.2 X-ray image of tooth decay. (BSIP/Photo Researchers, Inc.)

CAUSES AND MICROBIOLOGY OF DISEASE

If asked what the cause of cavities is, most people would say sugar, but this is incorrect. Sugar does not cause cavities, bacteria do. The relationship between sugar and bacteria is simple: When certain types of bacteria use sugar, they produce acid (lactic acid) as an end product. The acid, in turn, is damaging to the enamel of the teeth, slowly eating away at it. Unlike an acid burn on skin, however, there is no pain when the bacteria produce acid in the mouth because lactic acid is relatively weak and only a small amount is produced. A fun experiment to demonstrate the effect of acid is available at www.crest.com/crest_kids/eggsperiment.jsp.

Cavities are of greatest concern in children and adolescents. In this population, the tooth enamel is not yet fully developed and hardened. Since enamel protects teeth, it takes less acid to damage younger teeth than older, more mature teeth. Additionally, the bacterium that causes cavities is introduced into the mouth very early in life (ages one to three years), and diet determines whether this bacterium thrives or not.

The main bacterium that is responsible for cavity formation is *Streptococcus mutans* (Figure 6.3). The name was given by J.K. Clarke in 1924, who saw the bacteria as being more oval than round and thus believed that it was a mutant form of a streptococcus. *S. mutans* is a Gram-positive bacterium that sticks very well to teeth and other bacteria and is a primary component of plaque. In fact, a necessary factor for cavity formation is the presence of plaque. Brushing and flossing to remove plaque can directly lower the chances of getting cavities, even if lots of sweets are eaten.

There are two important properties of *S. mutans* that contribute to its **virulence**, or its ability to cause cavities. The first property is the stickiness of the bacterium. *S. mutans* produces several different substances that help it attach to surfaces. When *S. mutans* is grown in the presence of sucrose (table sugar), it produces glucans, which are polysaccharides made up of glucose sugars. Glucans help the bacterium stick to teeth and

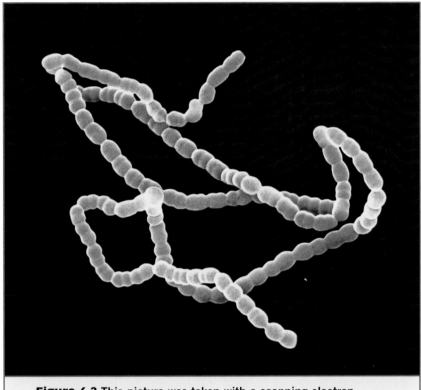

Figure 6.3 This picture was taken with a scanning electron micrograph and shows *Streptococcus mutans,* the bacterium that causes cavities, arranged in chains. (Dr. David Phillips/Visuals Unlimited)

to other bacteria. If the ability for *S. mutans* to make glucans is removed by making mutations, the bacterium is not able to incorporate into plaque normally and cannot cause cavities.

The second essential property for *S. mutans* to cause cavities is its ability to produce acid and survive in the presence of the low **pH**, or acidic, environment. Therefore, not only is *S. mutans* acidogenic (produces acid), but also it is acid tolerant (can tolerate acid). The bacterium is good at producing acid because it can **metabolize** a greater variety of sugars than nearly all other Gram-positive bacteria.

PREVENTION AND TREATMENT

It may not come as a surprise to hear that good oral hygiene can prevent cavities, but diet is an equally important factor. Dentists advise their patients not to eat too many sweets and not to drink sugary soft drinks. The average American drinks about two to three liters of liquid per day, and about half of that is in the form of soft drinks. Not only are most soft drinks acidic themselves (Coca-Cola and Pepsi contain phosphoric acid and have low pH values of 2.3), but the sugar in the drinks serves as a nutrient source for *S. mutans*.

In recent experiments, researchers mixed different soft drinks with extracted teeth and found that the enamel on the teeth showed etching and reduced hardness after only five minutes. Even the pH of plaque drops after the consumption of soft drinks. Because liquids can reach many more places in the mouth than food, such as small crevices and pockets where the bacteria hide, soft drinks should be considered as big a factor for cavities as candy. Dentists have assembled recommendations for the safer use of soft drinks, which are reproduced in Table 6.1.

Table 6.1 Recommendations for the Safer Use of Soft Drinks (from *Journal of Dentistry*, 2006)

1. Always follow the manufacturer's instructions on usage and dilution.
2. Ideally serve only at mealtimes.
3. Keep drinking times short.
4. Use a straw whenever possible.
5. Cooled drinks have less erosive potential.
6. Drinks should not be added to bottles, nor given at night time.
7. Drinks should not be swished around the mouth or held in contact with tooth surfaces.
8. Avoid tooth brushing immediately following consumption of an acidic drink.
9. Finish meals with something to neutralize any acids, e.g. cheese or milk
10. Low erosive beverages may be a valuable alternative to other acidic soft drinks.

Believe it or not, one of the best defenses against cavities is saliva. Saliva acts as a buffer against the acid that destroys our teeth. In fact, within 20 to 30 minutes after drinking low-acid drinks, the pH of oral plaque returns to normal values. If soft drinks and foods high in sugar are consumed regularly, however, the ability of saliva to work as a buffer decreases. This is why it is best to drink soft drinks only at mealtimes and not frequently throughout the day. People who have xerostomia (dry mouth) can't produce the normal amount of saliva. These people are much more prone to developing cavities, which further demonstrates the importance of saliva in maintaining good oral health.

In addition to normal brushing and flossing, fluoride treatment is extremely important to prevent cavities. Although the exact way in which fluoride works is still not clear, it is known that fluoride improves the acid resistance of enamel on teeth. Fluoride is an important treatment after permanent teeth erupt, or come in, (at about age six) when the teeth are still hardening. In many elementary schools, fluoride treatment is given weekly in the form of a mouthwash. Because fluoride is so important for oral health, most municipal water sources have a small amount of fluoride added, known as fluoridation.

Even when good oral hygiene is practiced, cavities may still develop and this necessitates a visit to the dentist. The standard treatment for cavities is for the dentist to drill (Figure 6.4) within the cavity to remove the bacteria and then fill the hole with a special material called **amalgam** or even colored filling material. The amalgam dries very fast and serves to seal the cavity so that bacteria can no longer gain access to this area. Because of the nerves and living tissue within teeth, drilling out cavities can be painful. Thankfully, there is medicine that a dentist can inject into the gums, called an anesthetic, to help stop the pain. If the cavity is very deep and reaches within the middle of the tooth, this is called an endodontic infection. In this case, a specialist called an **endodontist** must be visited to

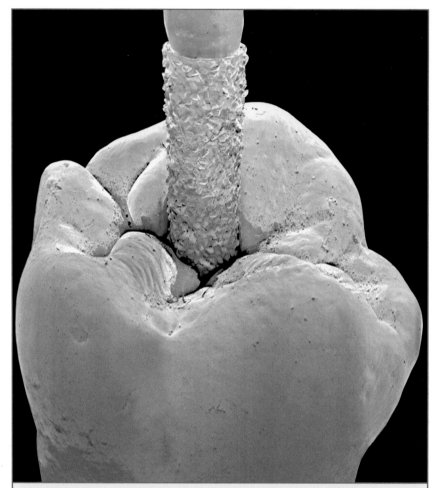

Figure 6.4 Colored scanning electron microscope image of a diamond-tipped dental drill (orange) drilling a hole into a tooth (blue). (Volker Steger/Photo Researchers, Inc.)

treat the infection. In the next chapter, we'll learn more about endodontic infections.

CURRENT RESEARCH

The study of cavities is called **cariology**. The field of cariology is exciting because of the real possibility for an effective therapy to prevent cavities. Two major research projects have resulted in significant discoveries in this field.

The first project was started by Dr. Jeffrey D. Hillman while at the Forsyth Institute, the University of Florida, and more recently at Oragenics Inc.

Dr. Hillman discovered that by mutating a certain gene in *S. mutans,* he was able to prevent the bacterium from producing lactic acid and consequently causing tooth decay and cavities. How does this help prevent cavities? *S. mutans* can be present in the mouth early in life when our teeth erupt, and it stays with us for the rest of our lives. Dr. Hillman used the genetically modified *S. mutans* that cannot produce lactic acid for something called **replacement therapy**. In replacement therapy, the idea is to replace or exchange one organism with a nearly identical, but less pathogenic, version of the same organism. In this case, the principle is to replace the cavity-causing *S. mutans* with the genetically modified *S. mutans* early in life so that the *S. mutans* that people have in their mouths is not able to cause cavities. In experiments with human volunteers, the genetically modified *S. mutans* remains in the mouth for many

PRODUCTS FOR ORAL HEALTH

Oragenics Inc. was started in 1996 in Alachua, Florida, by Dr. Jeffrey Hillman and Dr. Robert Zahradnik. The company specializes in oral health products that are the result of discoveries made by these two researchers over the past 25 years.

In addition to developing replacement therapy technology to prevent cavities, Oragenics is also testing a new type of antibiotic, called Mutacin 1140, that is actually produced by *S. mutans*. In addition, Oragenics is testing oral probiotic technology, a treatment that uses beneficial bacteria to promote dental health. More about the research and clinical testing that is being carried at Oragenics can be found at http://www.oragenics.com.

A Vaccine for Cavities?

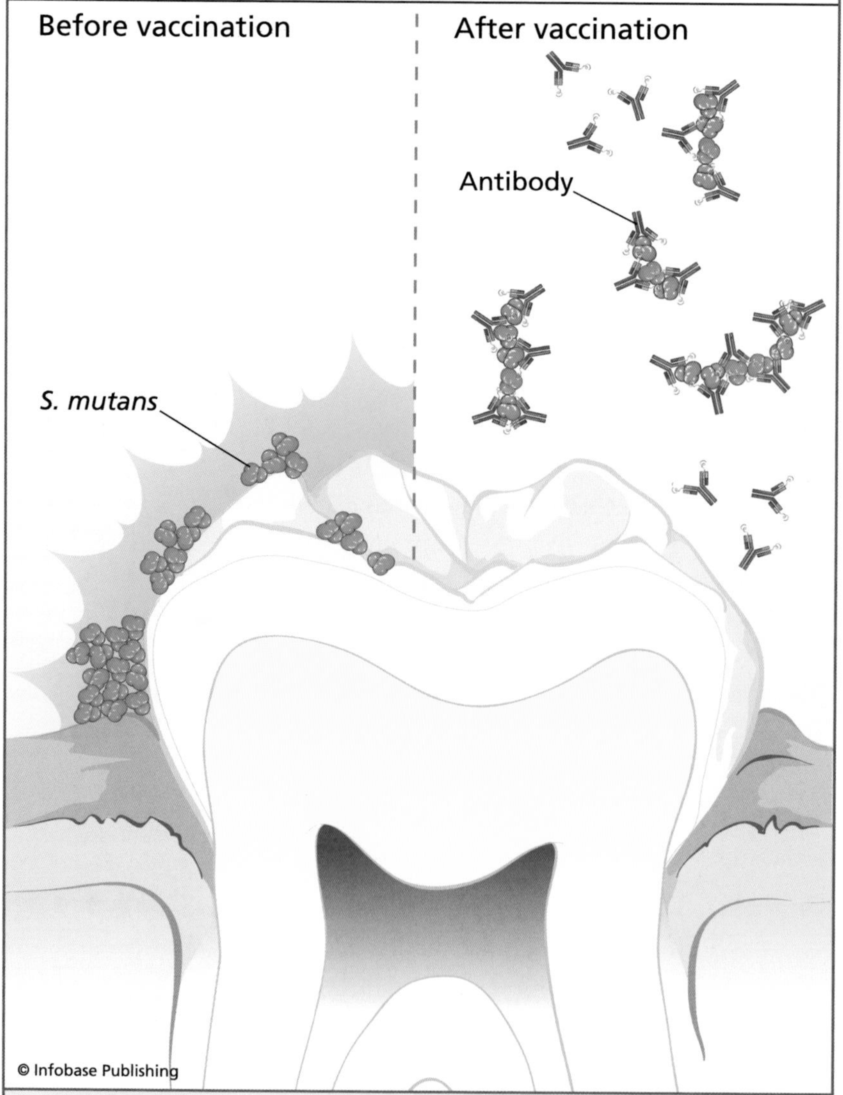

Before vaccination

After vaccination

Antibody

S. mutans

© Infobase Publishing

Figure 6.5 Shown here is how an experimental cavities vaccine might work. Antibodies specific for *S. mutans* might bind to bacteria, thereby preventing cells from attaching to teeth.

years and prevents the cavity-causing version of the bacterium from growing. In the future, a visit to the dentist may consist of the dentist swabbing teeth for a few minutes with the genetically modified *S. mutans* to prevent cavities for a lifetime.

The second exciting research area in the field of cariology is the development of a **vaccine** for cavities. The idea behind a vaccine is to use the natural immune system for protection. A vaccine consists of part of a pathogen that is injected into the body to stimulate an immune response. As discussed in Chapter 2, this part of a pathogen is called an antigen. The cavities vaccine uses part of *S. mutans*. It has been shown that antibodies directed against different parts of *S. mutans* could prevent its attachment to tooth surfaces and possibly its ability to produce acid from sugar (Figure 6.5). In laboratory experiments using different animals, it was found that administration of the vaccine could result in the production of antibodies in the mouth that were able to at least partially prevent cavities. In the next step, researchers used humans to test the vaccine. They gave the vaccine to young adults and found that the antibodies produced were able to delay the accumulation of *S. mutans* in the mouth. However, in order to be effective, the vaccine will have to be given to infants or young children (one to three years old) since this is the age when people are most prone to being colonized by *S. mutans*. Hence, if *S. mutans* can be prevented from invading the mouth from the start, the chances of getting cavities later in life are diminished significantly.

7

Endodontic Infections

As the name implies, endodontic infections occur within the tooth. The first step of the process is for bacteria to get into the dentin. This commonly occurs through cavities that erode into the dentin, but certain dental procedures, such as tooth wear caused by dental drilling, or dental cracks due to trauma can also give bacteria access to the inside of the tooth. The dentin is actually composed of thousands of small tubes called **dentinal tubules** (Figure 7.1). The dentinal tubules are approximately 1.0–2.5 micrometers in diameter, which is large enough for bacteria to travel through. Once bacteria have access to the dentinal tubules, they travel through them and into the pulp and root canal of the tooth. Within the pulp and root canal, bacteria and the responding immune cells produce toxic products that cause inflammation and swelling. Because the inside of the tooth contains living tissue, endodontic infections result in the destruction of the tissue that is essential for providing nutrients and blood to teeth.

Many people who have endodontic infections experience toothaches, sensitivity to cold or hot substances, swelling, and pain. These triggers often prompt a phone call or visit to the dentist, where the problem can be cared for. Sometimes, however, the infections are painless and the only way of detecting an endodontic problem is by discoloration of the tooth or by X-rays.

CAUSE AND MICROBIOLOGY OF DISEASE

Unlike periodontal disease and cavities, many different bacteria can cause endodontic infections. In fact, more than 200 different species of bacteria have been isolated from endodontic infections and often four or more species can be isolated from an individual root canal. It is

Dentinal Tubules within Dentin

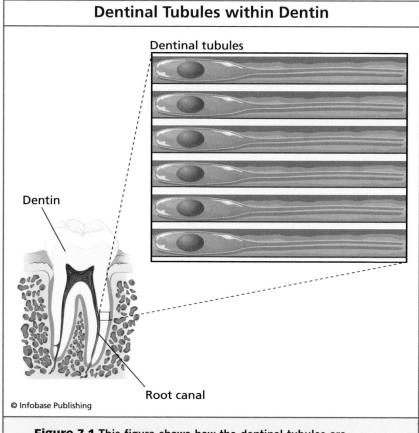

Dentinal tubules

Dentin

Root canal

© Infobase Publishing

Figure 7.1 This figure shows how the dentinal tubules are arranged within the dentin. The tubules extend from the pulp of the tooth outward.

difficult to tell whether all these bacteria can actually cause disease or if some just come along for the ride with other pathogens. Like the blood and lungs, the pulp and root canal are supposed to be sterile environments. Therefore, an infection of the root canal could also be caused by bacteria that are normally not pathogenic.

As it does in other oral diseases, the immune system plays an important role in endodontic infections. Within the pulp of the tooth is a large concentration of blood vessels. When bacteria enter the pulp system, immune cells sense these foreign invaders and an immune response is launched. This response to the initial invasion of the dental pulp usually results in swelling and pain. During the early immune response, the pulp tissue is damaged by the release of toxic products from both the bacteria and the immune system. Once the pulp is permanently damaged, the immune system cannot access the narrow and hidden environment of the root canal. Because antibodies and immune cells cannot penetrate, any remaining infecting bacteria are well protected and thrive. Thus, it is important for the immune system to be effective before the bacteria destroy the pulp.

Although a very large number of bacterial species have been isolated from endodontic infections, it is believed that only about 15 to 30 are actually responsible for causing disease. Three of the most common bacteria associated with endodontic infections are *P. gingivalis*, *Prevotella intermedia*, and *Peptostreptococcus micros*. Several common properties link these bacteria. First, they are able to bind to collagen, the major component of dentin. Second, the bacteria are able to penetrate and survive within dentin since this is an inherent barrier to the pulp. Finally, bacteria found in the pulp must be anaerobic, due to the lack of abundant oxygen within the interior of the teeth.

P. gingivalis is not only a successful periodontal pathogen, but also, for similar reasons, it appears to be a successful endodontic pathogen.

Prevotella intermedia is a Gram-negative bacterium in the shape of a rod that does not survive in the presence of oxygen. The bacterium possesses hemagglutinating activity, which means that it can bind red blood cells and potentially acquire nutrients from them. The LPS from bacteria such as *P. intermedia* has been shown to resist the action of host antibodies, allowing the bacteria to further escape the efforts of the immune system. In addition, *P. intermedia* can bind to hemoglobin, an important way for it to obtain iron. Of all the oral pathogens, *P. intermedia* is one of the most antibiotic resistant. This causes problems because *P. intermedia* may have the potential to pass along the antibiotic resistance trait to other bacteria it associates with. Indeed, this is one way in which very dangerous bacterial pathogens (such as *Mycobacterium tuberculosis* and *Bacillus anthracis*) become antibiotic resistant.

The third bacterium that plays a significant role in causing endodontic infections is *Peptostreptococcus micros. P. micros* is a Gram-positive bacterium that is also anaerobic but can tolerate some oxygen. An important virulence property of this bacterium is its ability to produce proteases that destroy tissue in the mouth. *P. micros* also produces a capsule, which is important for the bacterium to cause disease. Recall that a polysaccharide capsule protects bacteria from the immune system.

P. micros is also a systemic pathogen, which means that it can infect other sites in the body including the brain, vagina, and lungs. In these cases, the oral cavity may serve as an important **reservoir** where the bacteria persist.

PREVENTION AND TREATMENT

Because endodontic pathogens are usually part of the normal oral flora, the best way to prevent endodontic infections is by brushing and flossing to keep a healthy mouth. Teeth with unfilled cavities have a higher risk of developing endodontic infections than those without cavities. The same can be said for periodontal disease. When an endodontic infection does occur, a dentist will often refer the patient to an endodontist.

The most important goal of endodontic treatment is to save the tooth. A simple removal of the tooth would indeed eliminate the infection (since it is essentially contained within the tooth); however, **extraction** of a tooth means that an artificial tooth must be put in its place. Tooth extraction is a last resort if the dentist feels that the infection cannot be eliminated with other procedures. Although it is possible to replace the missing tooth with an artificial implant, nothing is better than natural teeth.

How does an endodontist save a tooth? From a practical point of view, it is the endodontist's job to eliminate bacteria and dead tissue from the root canal system and prevent the bacteria from reinfecting the area. Root canals are the most common endodontic procedure performed, with nearly 16 million procedures in the United States each year.

After the endodontist takes X-rays to determine the severity of the infection, he or she will drill into the tooth in order to gain access to the pulp tissue. The drill that is used is similar to the one used for filling cavities. After the hole is drilled, an endodontist uses an endodontic file. The endodontic file is used to clean the inside of the tooth by inserting and removing it from the canal to essentially scrape out bacteria and dead tissue (imagine a pipe cleaner cleaning the inside of a narrow pipe). After the root canal has been scraped, it is further cleaned with a disinfectant solution to kill any remaining bacteria. The root canal is then dried with a special absorbent paper and filled with rubberlike material. The original hole that was drilled is finally sealed much the way a cavity is filled. All this might sound like a simple cleaning exercise, but now imagine doing all this in the small space of the mouth within a root canal that is no more than one millimeter (.04 in.) in diameter. This is why an endodontist must train for two more years after dental school.

A common myth is that root canal treatment is painful. In fact, root canal treatment helps relieve pain, not cause it. Since the pain is caused by the inflammation and damaged tissue within the pulp, removal of the tissue during treatment relieves pain. With the latest anesthetics and techniques, an endodontist is able to minimize the pain felt by a patient. However, before modern techniques and anesthetics, a root canal was extremely painful.

CURRENT RESEARCH

Endodontic infections can be caused by many different bacteria, and current research is directed at identifying the multi-

ENDODONTICS

The history of endodontics began in the second or third century B.C. A skull found in the Israeli desert had a bronze wire in one of the teeth. The wire may have been used to remove infected pulp. However, modern endodontics really began much later. In the early 1700s, Pierre Fauchard (1678–1761) was the first to accurately describe dental pulp and how to remove the pulp tissue during infection. Up until that time, it was believed that "tooth worms" were responsible for toothaches caused by the infections. In 1838, Edwin Maynard of Washington, D.C., used a filed watch spring as the first root canal instrument. Perhaps the greatest advance came in 1895 when the German dentist Otto Walkhoff took the first dental X-ray.

tude of types. Because many of the bacteria cannot be grown on standard laboratory media, researchers use molecular tools to identify bacteria straight from the mouth. A very sensitive and specific method that is employed is called **polymerase chain reaction** (PCR). PCR was discovered in the 1980s by Dr. Kary Mullis and today is used in nearly every research laboratory in the world. In 1993, Dr. Mullis received the Nobel Prize in Chemistry for his discovery.

In PCR, DNA is amplified to make more copies of itself (Figure 7.2). The strength of the technique is that the researcher can specify exactly which gene or genes should be amplified. Thus, in a bacterial chromosome, there is one copy of each gene. If researchers were interested in looking at one particular gene, they would need to generate more of it; a relatively large quantity of DNA is required for detection of the gene, DNA sequencing, and cloning. How does PCR help identify unknown bacteria? As with all organisms, bacteria harbor some genes that are very similar among all bacteria. These genes are said to be well conserved, meaning their properties

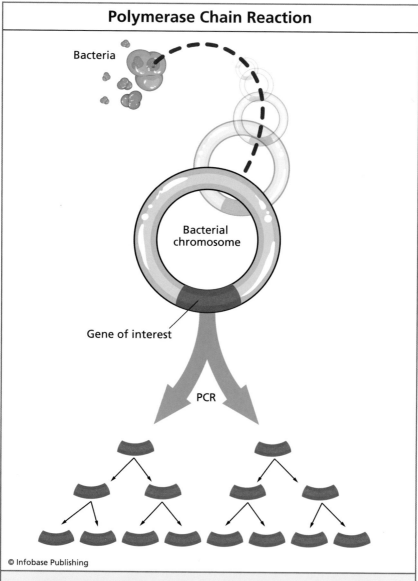

Figure 7.2 This picture shows how the polymerase chain reaction works. A single gene of interest or fragment of DNA can be amplified with multiple rounds of the reaction.

have not changed very much over time. However, even well-conserved genes do differ slightly from each other and each bacterium has a DNA sequence that is unique to them. This characteristic DNA sequence is called a **DNA fingerprint**. For example, the *P. gingivalis* DNA sequence might read "GTCC-**GA**TGCTCG," while the *F. nucleatum* DNA sequence would be "GTCC**AC**TGCTCG." For endodontic infections, researchers have taken samples from infected root canals and performed PCR on the collected bacteria. The products that are obtained from PCR are then sequenced and the fingerprint is determined and compared to a database of all known bacteria. In this way, researchers have determined that nearly 200 different bacterial species could be found in endodontic infections, without having to grow all of them in the laboratory.

Unlike many diseases, such as cancer and multiple sclerosis, infectious diseases of the mouth are highly preventable. With proper oral hygiene and regular visits to a dentist, plaque buildup and overgrowth of pathogenic microorganisms, which ultimately lead to disease, can be prevented. And a healthy mouth will mean a more healthy body. Continued research efforts in the field of oral biology will help us better understand how some oral bacteria can cause disease and how we can more effectively prevent and treat oral diseases.

Glossary

aerobic—Using oxygen for growth and metabolism.

agar—A gelling agent used in bacterial growth media that allows liquids to become a gel-like solid.

alveolar process—The bony material below a tooth that helps anchor the tooth in place by connecting to the periodontal ligament.

amalgam—The material that is used to fill a cavity.

anaerobic—Not requiring any oxygen for growth.

antigen—Part of an organism that is foreign to our bodies and stimulates an immune response.

asexual organisms—Living creatures (usually bacteria) that are neither male nor female, and therefore do not reproduce by exchanging genetic material.

biofilm—A complex community of microorganisms living together and attached to a surface.

capsule—A structure that surrounds or encapsulates many bacteria and may serve to protect them from harsh conditions or to assist with adherence to surfaces.

cariology—The study of cavities.

cementum—The part of a tooth that anchors the tooth into the jawbone.

collagen—The strong connective tissue that is found in tendons, cartilage, and bones.

collagenase—An enzyme produced by some bacteria that breaks down the connective tissue collagen.

colonies—Masses of bacteria that arise from a single cell on solid growth media.

colonization—The act of attaching to and inhabiting a surface.

conjugation—The process of DNA transfer from one bacterial cell to another.

connective tissue—Biological material that serves to support and bind together organs.

crown—The part of a tooth that is above the gums.

culturing—The act of growing bacteria in a laboratory.

curettes—Tools used by a dentist to remove plaque from teeth.

cytokine—Proteins that are made by cells that alter the properties and behavior of other cells.

cytosol—The interior of a cell that contains the cell's inner components, or "guts."

dentin—The layer of the tooth just below the enamel.

dentinal tubules—The branching tubes in the dentin that extend outward from the pulp.

dissemination—The process by which a pathogen is transmitted from one host to another.

DNA fingerprint—A characteristic sequence of nucleic acid bases (A, G, C, T) that is unique to and defines a given bacterial species.

dormant—A state of inactivity and slowed metabolism, similar to hibernation.

enamel—The outside coating of a tooth.

endodontic infections—Infections that occur within the pulp of the tooth.

endodontist—A dentist who specializes in treating endodontic infections.

endoplasmic reticulum—In a eukaryotic cell, the structure on which ribosomes reside.

extracellular—The environment outside of a cell.

extraction—Surgical removal of a tooth.

flagella—Flexible rope-like structures that help bacteria swim and move in different environments.

genome—The complete DNA material of an organism.

genus—The designation for a group of organisms highly related to each other.

gingiva—The gums.

gingivitis—Gum disease.

glucan—A general term for sugar or polysaccharide.

Gram negative—Bacteria that appear pink after the Gram stain procedure due to their thin peptidoglycan cell wall.

Gram positive—Bacteria that appear purple after the Gram stain procedure due to their thick peptidoglycan cell wall.

growth media—The food and nutrients on which bacteria grow in the laboratory.

hemagglutination—The clumping together of red blood cells.

hemolysin—A bacterial toxin that is able to destroy red blood cells.

Glossary

hemolysis—The act of lysing, or killing, a red blood cell.

host—The organism, usually a human, that a pathogen lives in or on.

hydrated—Containing water.

immuno-compromised—A state where an individual's immune system is weakened, usually by an infection or disease.

incubate—To allow microorganisms to grow in the lab under favorable growth conditions.

inflammation—The process whereby immune cells and chemicals accumulate at the site of infection and result in swelling and redness.

inner membrane—The phospholipid-containing structure around a Gram-negative cell.

invasin—A protein that a pathogen uses to enter into a host cell.

lectin—A protein that binds to a specific type of sugar.

leukotoxin—A bacterial toxin that is able to destroy white blood cells.

lipid A—The innermost portion of lipopolysaccharide (LPS) that anchors it into the outer membrane of Gram-negative bacteria; composed of lipid.

lipopolysaccharide (LPS)—The outer part of the outer membrane of Gram-negative bacteria; composed of lipid and sugars.

localized—Found only at a specific location.

macroscopic—Large enough to be seen with the naked eye.

metabolize—To utilize a nutrient source for growth and maintenance.

microbiologist—A professional who studies organisms too small to be seen with the naked eye.

migration—The act of moving throughout the body and occupying a new environment.

mucins—Large proteins in saliva that give it hydrating properties.

normal flora—The community of microorganisms that is found in an environment during good health.

nucleoid—The region of the bacterial cell cytosol that contains the chromosome.

O-antigen—The outermost portion of lipopolysaccharide; composed of sugars linked together in chains.

oligosaccharide core—The central portion of lipopolysaccharide that links the O-antigen to lipid A; composed of sugars.

organelles—Discrete structures that carry out specific functions within a a cell.

outer membrane—The outermost layer of a Gram-negative cell that contains both phospholipids and lipopolysaccharide.

pathogen—An organism that can cause disease.

peptide—A short sequence of amino acids linked together in a chain.

peptidoglycan—Chemical that makes up a bacterial cell wall; composed of a mixture of amino acids and sugars.

periodontal debridement—The process of removing plaque and decay from teeth.

periodontal ligament—The connective tissue that connects the tooth to the underlying bone.

periodontium—The tissues that surround the teeth; made up of the gingiva, the cementum, the periodontal ligament, and the alveolar process.

persistent—A state where a pathogen remains in an environment for a prolonged period of time.

pH—The measure of how acidic or basic a substance is; acids have low pH values and bases have high pH values.

phagocytes—Cells of the immune system that are able to engulf pathogens and parts of them.

phospholipid bilayer—The composition of cell membranes; made up of phosphate groups attached to lipid molecules.

pili—Bacterial hair-like projections that are made of protein and aid in attachment to surfaces and other bacteria.

plaque—The bacterial biofilm that accumulates on teeth.

polymerase chain reaction (PCR)—The method by which the amount of genetic material (DNA) can be selectively increased.

polymicrobial infection—An infection caused by more than one microorganism.

probe—The tool used to determine the depth of a periodontal pocket.

proteinaceous—Composed of proteins.

pulp—The center of the tooth, containing living tissue.

Glossary

replacement therapy—The practice of using one organism to replace a more pathogenic form of itself in order to prevent or treat disease.

reservoir—A location in the body or environment where bacteria can live in balance with the host, and serves as a source for subsequent infections.

resolution—The ability to distinguish two objects as separate entities.

ribosome—The structure on which amino acids are synthesized into a protein.

root—The part of a tooth that is below the gums.

saliva—The liquid produced in our mouths by the salivary glands that helps to maintain good oral health.

salivary antibody—Proteins in the mouth that are directed against specific pathogens.

salivary glands—The organs in the mouth that produce saliva.

scalers—Tools used to remove plaque from teeth.

secretion systems—Components that bacteria use to export material from the inside of their cells to the outside.

sialidase—An enzyme produced by some bacteria that breaks apart specific types of sugars.

species—The designation for organisms that are biologically identical to each other.

transpeptidation—Linking together sugar chains with peptides.

vaccine—A substance that can boost the immune response and protect us from subsequent infection by a specific pathogen.

virulence—The ability to cause disease.

xerostomia—A condition of dry mouth.

Dodds, M.W., D.A. Johnson, and C.K. Yeh. "Health Benefits of Saliva: A Review." *Journal of Dentistry* 33 (2005): 223–233.

Ehrlich, A.B., H.O. Torres, and D. Bird. *Essentials of Dental Assisting*, 2nd Ed. Philadelphia: W.B. Saunders, 1996.

Holt, S.C., and J.L. Ebersole. "*Porphyromonas Gingivalis, Treponema Denticola, and Tannerella Forsythia*: The "Red Complex," A Prototype Polybacterial Pathogenic Consortium in Periodontitis." *Periodontology* 38 (2000): 72–122.

Kassab, M.M., and R.E. Cohen. "The Etiology and Prevalence of Gingival Recession." *Journal of American Dental Association* 134 (2003): 220–225.

Loesche, W.J. "Role of *Streptococcus Mutans* in Human Dental Decay." *Microbiology Review* 50 (1986): 353–380.

Lovegrove, J.M. "Dental Plaque Revisited: Bacteria Associated with Periodontal Disease." *Journal of the New Zealand Society of Periodontology* 87 (2004): 7–21.

Marsh, P.D. "Dental Plaque as a Microbial Biofilm." *Caries Research* 38 (2004): 204–211.

Mitchell, T.J. "The Pathogenesis of Streptococcal Infections: From Tooth Decay to Meningitis." *Nature Reviews Microbiology* 1 (2003): 219–230.

Newman, M.G., H.H. Takei, and F.A. Carranza. *Carranza's Clinical Periodontology*, 9th ed. Philadelphia: W.B. Saunders Co., 2002.

Nishihara, T., and T. Koseki. "Microbial Etiology of Periodontitis." *Periodontology* 36 (2004): 14–26.

Preshaw, P.M., R.A. Seymour, and P.A. Heasman. "Current Concepts in Periodontal Pathogenesis." *Dental Update* 31 (2004): 570–572, 574–578.

Roberts, A. "Bacteria in the Mouth." *Dental Update* 32 (2005): 134–136, 139–140, 142.

Roberts, F.A., and R.P. Darveau. "Beneficial Bacteria of the Periodontium." *Periodontology* 30 (2000): 40–50.

Roberts, G.L. "Fusobacterial Infections: An Underestimated Threat." *British Journal of Biomedical Science* 57 (2000): 156–162.

Rogers, A.H. "Why Be Down in the Mouth? Three Decades of Research in Oral Microbiology." *Australian Dental Journal* 50 (2005): 2–5.

Russell, M.W., N.K. Childers, S.M. Michalek, D.J. Smith, and M.A. Taubman. "A Caries Vaccine? The State of the Science of Immunization Against Dental Caries." *Caries Research* 38 (2004): 230–235.

Bibliography

Salvi, G.E., C.A. Ramseier, M. Kandylaki, L. Sigrist, E. Awedowa, and N.P. Lang. "Experimental Gingivitis in Cigarette Smokers: A Clinical and Microbiological Study." *Journal of Clinical Peridontology* 32 (2005): 441–447.

Satcher, D.S. "Surgeon General's Report on Oral Health." *Public Health Reports* 115 (2000): 489–90.

Sela, M.N. "Role of *Treponema Denticola* in Periodontal Diseases." *Critical Reviews in Oral Biology and Medicine* 12 (2001): 399–413.

Seow, W.K., and K.M. Thong. "Erosive Effects of Common Beverages on Extracted Premolar Teeth." *Australian Dental Journal* 50 (2005): 173–178.

Tahmassebi, J.F., M.S. Duggal, G. Malik-Kotru, and M.E. Curzon. "Soft Drinks and Dental Health: A Review of the Current Literature." *Journal of Dentistry* 34 (2006): 2–11.

Tatakis, D.N., and P.S. Kumar. "Etiology and Pathogenesis of Periodontal Diseases." *Dental Clinics of North America* 49 (2005): 491–516

Van Eygen, I., B.V. Vannet, and H. Wehrbein. "Influence of a Soft Drink with Low pH on Enamel Surfaces: An *In Vitro* Study." *American Journal of Orthodontics and Dentofacial Orthopedics* 128 (2005): 372–377.

Zero, D.T. "Sugars—The Arch Criminal?" *Caries Research* 38 (2004): 277–285.

Further Resources

Books

Day, N. *Killer Superbugs: The Story of Drug-Resistant Diseases.* Berkeley Heights, N.J.: Enslow Publishers, 2001.

De Kruif, P. *Microbe Hunters.* San Diego, Calif.: Harcourt Brace, 1996.

Favor, L.J. *Bacteria,* 1st ed. New York: The Rosen Publishing Group, 2004.

Gest, H. *Microbes: An Invisible Universe.* Washington, DC: ASM Press, 2003.

Kendall, B.L., and NetLibrary Inc. *Opportunities in Dental Care Careers,* Rev. ed. Chicago: VGM Career Horizons, 2001.

Nweeia, M.T. *The Whole Tooth: Answers to the Questions You Always Wanted to Ask Your Dentist.* Honolulu, HI: Randall Morita Design, 1999.

Reh, B.D. *Germs.* Detroit, Mich.: Greenhaven Press, 2005.

Rickert, J.A. *Exploring Careers in Dentistry,* Rev. ed. New York: Rosen Publishing Group, 1997.

Satcher, D.S. "Surgeon General's Report on Oral Health." *Public Health Reports* 115 (2000): 489–490.

Sherman, J. *The War Against Germs,* 1st ed. New York: The Rosen Publishing Group, 2004.

Wynbrandt, J. *The Excruciating History of Dentistry: Toothsome Tales & Oral Oddities from Babylon to Braces.* New York: St. Martin's Press, 1998.

Web Sites

American Dental Association
http://www.ada.org/
This site provides important information about practicing good oral hygiene.

American Society for Microbiology
http://www.asm.org
This organization provides valuable resources about bacteria and microorganisms.

The Forsyth Institute
http://www.forsyth.org/
This institute is a leader in oral biology research.

Further Resources

International Association for Dental Research
http://www.iadr.org/
This association provides valuable resources about oral care and research in dentistry.

The National Institute of Dental and Craniofacial Research
http://www.nidcr.nih.gov/
This site provides information about dental research funding in America.

The National Institutes of Health
http://www.nih.gov/
The site provides information about grants and research funding in America.

The Surgeon General's Report on Oral Health, May 2000
http://www.surgeongeneral.gov/library/oralhealth/
This site contains that full report on oral health in America released by Dr. David Satcher.

Index

Index

Index

of *Porphyromonas gingivalis*, 54
of *Prevotella intermedia*, 70
localized infection, 34, 78
LPS. *See* lipopolysaccharide
lysozyme, 37

macroscopic structures, 20, 78
magnet, as lens for electron microscope, 29
magnification, 27
Maynard, Edwin, 73
men, gingivitis and, 40
metabolizing, of sugar, 61
microbiologist, work of, 26
microbiology, 10–31
  bacteria as complex organism, 10–20, *14*
  bacterial causes of disease, 21–25
  bacterial DNA sequencing, 30–31
  of cavities, 60–61
  of endodontic infections, 68–71
  of gingivitis, 41–44
  laboratory studies of bacteria, 25–31
  of mouth, 37–39
  naming of bacteria, 20–21
  of periodontal disease, 49–50
microscopes, 26–29
migration, 23, 78
molar, 33, *34*, 58
mouth
  anatomy of, 32–37
  as bacterial entry point to body, 39
  as ideal bacterial environment, *22*, 32–39
  microbiology of, 37–39
  and migration of bacteria, 23

mouthwash, 45
mucins, 37, 78
Mullis, Kary, 73
Mutacin 1140, 65
mutation, 31, 57
Mycobacterium tuberculosis
  antibiotic resistance, 71
  dissemination by, 24
  dormancy, 23

N-acetylglucosamine (NAG), 15
N-acetylmuramic acid (NAM), 15
naming, of bacteria, 20–21
National Institute of Dental and Craniofacial Research (NIDCR), 39
normal flora, 37, 71, 78
nucleoid, 19, 78
nutrients, for bacteria, 23, 29

O-antigen, 18, 78
objective lens, 27
oligosaccharide core, 18, 79
Oragenics, Inc., 65
oral bacteria. *See* plaque
oral health products, 65
oral hygiene
  for endodontic infection prevention, 75
  for gingivitis prevention, 45
  for periodontal disease treatment, 56
organelles, 10, 19, 79
outer membrane, 18, 79

pain
  early stages of cavities, 60
  endodontic infections, 70
  gingivitis, 40
  root canal procedure, 72
pathogen
  bacteria as, 21
  battle with host, 25

definition, 79
migration of, 23
PCR. *See* polymerase chain reaction
penicillin, 15
peptide
  definition, 79
  histatin, 37
  and peptidoglycan, 15
peptidoglycan
  components of, 15
  definition, 79
  of Gram-negative bacteria, 18
  and Gram staining, 16
Peptostreptococcus micros, 41, 70, 71
periapical cyst, 49
periodontal debridement, 55, 56, 79
periodontal disease, 47–57, *49*
  aggressive periodontitis, 54
  bacteria, 51–54, *52*
  chronic periodontitis, 50–54
  microbiology of, 49–50
  prevention/treatment, 54–56, *55*
  research, 56–57
periodontal ligament, *36, 48*
  definition, 79
  and periodontal disease, 47
  and periodontium, 35
periodontal pocket, 47, 50, 56
periodontist, 54–55
periodontitis
  aggressive, 54
  chronic, 50–54
  gingivitis and, 45
periodontium, 35, 79
persistent gingivitis, 45
petri dish, 30

pH
  definition, 79
  effect of saliva on, 63
  effect of soft drinks on,
    62
  Streptococcus mutans
    and, 61
phagocytes, 37, 79
phospholipid bilayer,
    15–16, 79
photon, 27
pili, *14*
  definition, 11, 79
  and periodontal disease
    research, 57
  of *Porphyromonas gingi-
    valis*, 53
plaque, *38*
  bacteria in, 37
  definition, 79
  developmental process,
    38
  and endodontic infection
    prevention, 75
  first microscopic exami-
    nation of, 26
  and gingivitis, 41–45, *43*
  and periodontal disease,
    50
  Streptococcus mutans, 60
polymerase chain reaction
    (PCR), 73–75, *74*, 79
polymicrobial infection,
    50–51, 79
polysaccharide, 53. *See
    also* lipopolysaccharide
    (LPS)
polysaccharide capsule. *See*
    capsule
Porphyromonas gingivalis
  and endodontic infec-
    tions, 70
  and periodontal disease,
    53–54
  and periodontal disease
    research, 57
pregnancy, gingivitis and,
    40
premolar, 33, *34*

prevention
  of cavities, 60, 62–63,
    65–67
  of endodontic infections,
    71, 75
  of gingivitis, 45
  of periodontal disease,
    54–56
Prevotella intermedia,
    70–71
Prevotella sp., 41
probe, 55, 79
prokaryotes, 10
protease, 54, 71
protein
  and cell layer, 16
  in eukaryotic cells, 19–20
  and gingivitis, 42
  and Gram-negative bac-
    teria, 18
  invasin, 23
pulp, 35, *36*, 79
  and beginning of end-
    odontic infections, 68
  and endodontic infec-
    tions, 69–70
  endodontic infection
    treatment, 72
  and endodontics, 73
pulp chamber, 35

red blood cell, 53
replacement therapy, 65,
    67, 80
research
  on bacteria, 25–31
  on cavities, 64–67
  Forsyth Institute and, 50
  funding for, 39
  on gingivitis, 45–46
  as key to containing oral
    health epidemic, 9
  on periodontal disease,
    56–57
research microbiologist, 26
reservoir, 71, 80
resolution
  definition, 80
  of electron microscope, 29

of light microscope, 27,
    29
ribosome, 19–20, 80
root, 34, *36*, 80
root canal (anatomy), 35
  and beginning of end-
    odontic infections,
    68
  and PCR, 75
root canal (procedure)
  earliest, 73
  endodontic infection
    treatment, 72
root planing, 56

safranin, 16
saliva, 35–37, 63, 80
salivary antibody, 37, 80
salivary glands, 35, 80
Sanger, Frederick, 30
Satcher, David, 8, 9
scalers/scaling, 55–56, 80
scanning electron micro-
    scope, 28, 29, 64
secretion systems, 16, 80
sequencing of genome. *See*
    DNA sequencing
shapes, of bacteria, *13*
sialidase, 51, 80
slide (microscope), 27
smoking
  and chronic periodonti-
    tis, 47–54
  and gingivitis, 44
soft drinks
  and cavity prevention,
    62, 63
  recommendations for
    safer use of, 62*t*
species, 20–21, 80
spindle, 51
spirillum, *13*
spirochete, 53
stage (microscope), 27
Staphylococcus, 21
starch, 36
Streptococcus mutans, 61
  and cavities, 60
  and cavity prevention, 62

Index

cavity-prevention
    research, 65–67
Forsyth Institute's
    research, 50
Jeffrey Hillman's research,
    65–66
and plaque formation, 38
vaccine research, *66,* 67
Streptococcus pyogenes, 25
Streptococcus sp., 41
structure, of bacteria,
    10–20, *14*
sucrose, 60
sugar, 60, 62
surgery, for periodontal
    disease treatment, 56
swelling, endodontic infec-
    tions and, 70
systemic pathogen, 71

Tanner, Anne, 51
Tanneralla forsythensis, 51
T-cell, 43
tobacco. *See* smoking
tongue, as reservoir for
    bacteria, 35
tools. *See* dental tools
tooth. *See also* cavities;
    endodontic infections

anatomy, 32–35, *36*
    names of, *34*
toothbrush. *See also* brush-
    ing
    dissemination of bacteria
    by sharing, 25
    evolution of, 42
tooth decay. *See also* cavities
    prevalence of, 8–9
    X-ray image, *59*
toxin, bacterial, 25
transmission electron
    microscope, 14, 28, 29
transpeptidation, 15, 80
treatment
    of cavities, 62–64
    of endodontic infections,
    71–72
    of gingivitis, 45
    of periodontal disease,
    54–56, *55*
Treponema denticola, 52, 53
turbidity, 30

ultrasonic scaler, 56
ultrasound, 55, 56

vaccine
    anti-cavity, *66,* 67

definition, 80
Vibrio cholerae
    dissemination of, 25
    naming of, 21
virulence
    definition, 80
    of *Streptococcus mutans,*
    60–61

Walkhoff, Otto, 73
wavelength, of electron, 29
white blood cell. *See* leu-
    kocyte
wisdom tooth, 33, *34*

xerostomia
    and cavity prevention, 63
    definition, 80
    and saliva, 37
X-ray
    endodontic infection
    treatment, 72
    first use in dentistry, 73
    tooth decay image, *59*

Yersin, Alexandre, 21
Yersinia pestis, 21

About the Author

Scott C. Kachlany, Ph.D., is assistant professor of oral biology and micro-biology and molecular genetics at the University of Medicine and Dentistry of New Jersey. He received his B.S. in microbiology from Cornell University in 1997 and his Ph.D. in microbiology from Columbia University College of Physicians and Surgeons in 2001.

About the Consulting Editor

Hilary Babcock, M.D., M.P.H., is an instructor in medicine in the Infectious Diseases Division of Washington University School of Medicine and the medical director of Occupational Infection Control at Barnes-Jewish Hospital and St. Louis Children's Hospital. She is a graduate of Brown University and holds an M.D. from the University of Texas Southwestern Medical School, as well as an M.P.H. from St. Louis University. She has lectured, taught, and written extensively about infectious diseases, their treatment, and their prevention. She is a member of numerous medical associations and is board certified in infectious disease. She lives in St. Louis, Missouri.